D0187721

The
Balancing
Act

A Daily Rediscovery of Grace

ROBERT SCHNASE

ABINGDON PRESS
Nashville, Tennessee

THE BALANCING ACT

Copyright © 2009 by Robert Schnase

All rights reserved.
No part of this work may be reproduced or transmitted in any form or by any means, electronic or mechanical, including photocopying and recording, or by any information storage or retrieval system, except as may be expressly permitted by the 1976 Copyright Act or in writing from the publisher. Requests for permission can be addressed to Abingdon Press, P.O. Box 801, 201 Eighth Avenue South, Nashville, TN 37202-0801, or e-mailed to permissions@abingdonpress.com.

This book is printed on acid-free paper.

ISBN 978-1-426-70283-9

All Scripture quotations unless noted otherwise are taken from the New Revised Standard Version of the Bible, copyright 1989, Division of Christian Education of the National Council of the Churches of Christ in the United States of America. Used by permission. All rights reserved.

Scripture quotations from *THE MESSAGE*. Copyright © by Eugene H. Peterson 1993, 1994, 1995, 1996, 2000, 2001, 2002. Used by permission of NavPress Publishing Group.

Please note, italics have been added for emphasis to some Scripture quotations by the author.

09 10 11 12 13 14 15 16 17 18—10 9 8 7 6 5 4 3 2 1
MANUFACTURED IN THE UNITED STATES OF AMERICA

TABLE OF CONTENTS

Embracing Change

Letting Go

Reaching Out

In Appreciation

My thanks goes to Erin Horner, Amy Forbus, and Sherry Habben who keep the FivePractices.org website and blog fresh and inviting, and to my friend Judy Davidson and Abingdon editor Susan Salley for their constant encouragement, gentle correction, and unceasing support. Without these colleagues and friends, there would be no Five Practices blog and no compiling of the weblogs into this book. Also, I offer my thanks to Dala Dunn and Dick Curry who keep me on top of my day job so that I can fill the smallest gaps of time with writing. My special thanks to my family—Esther, Karl, and Paul—who tolerate the sound of fingertips tapping on the laptop at all hours of the day and night. Above all, I give God thanks for the rich privilege of serving alongside the pastors and laity of the Missouri Conference in the tough and joyful task of ministry.

INTRODUCTION

"So here's what I want you to do, God helping you:
Take your everyday, ordinary life—your sleeping, eating,
going-to-work, and walking-around life—and place it
before God as an offering. Embracing what God
does for you is the best thing you can do for him. Don't
become so well-adjusted to your culture that you fit into it
without even thinking. Instead, fix your attention on God.
You'll be changed from the inside out."
(Romans 12:1-2, *THE MESSAGE*)

Threads of grace interlace our everyday experiences. Each day the holy intertwines with the mundane, our common lives are touched by the new creation offered us in Christ. Focused on work, family, routine, health, worry, finances, necessity, and constant activity, and distracted by the blur and sound of television, video, Internet, podcasts, MP3s, radio, and commercial culture, we easily overlook the movement of spirit and the stirrings of grace. Living in fast-forward, we neglect the interior life and the spiritual journey and misperceive the signs of God's presence. Intimations of God's love go unnoticed and God's activity, undetected.

The Balancing Act: A Daily Rediscovery of Grace sharpens our perception. The stories cause us to look afresh at our living-breathingng-crying-laughing life for the striking of God's ...erruption, the unexpected traces of God's love. It ...ne our own faith journeys through the perspective of ...pic each day taken from everyday life experiences.

...e brief stories stimulate interior conversations with God. ...ey provoke rich discussions with colleagues, coworkers, and companions about the spiritual journey, the interior life, and the intertwining of faith and the daily events through which God speaks to us. These stories help us support one another, listen for God's calling, and talk one another into a greater boldness for Christ. These draw us out of ourselves and help us see the world through God's eyes. They provoke personal reflection, causing us to sift through our own experiences to perceive the presence, guidance, and sustenance of God's Spirit.

All of us have our experiences of life: the daily dialogues, habits, routines, encounters, and practices that shape us as well as the unexpected interruptions, painful disappointments, and extravagant delights that catch us by surprise. It's a rare privilege to take the time to reflect upon our experiences, to sift through them for meaning, to see in them brief glimpses of the grace of God. The sweep of time allows us to perceive purpose more clearly and to see the significance of our part in the larger story of God's creating and recreating activity. Our personal stories of pride, brokenness, anger, doubt, forgiveness, humor, faith, redemption, striving, and serving intertwine with the stories of millions of other Christian travelers past and present. Each of our journeys replicates in small letters the capital challenges of the ages—sin, grace, faith, calling, service, resurrection. The threads of grace evident in our own lives intertwine with those of others to form the fabric of faith extending back for millennia and forward to eternity.

These stories focus on everyday events; they are the raw stuff of daily life. They invite us to notice God, and the people God places before us, with greater attentiveness and receptivity. Bridging the chasm between what we believe and what we do requires the hard work of daily reflection, and the intentional rediscovery of grace in everyday life.

Jesus noticed seeds spilled on pathways, birds making nests, money tables in temples, figs on trees, flour baskets brimming over, leftover bread, branches on vines. Jesus was captivated by beauty, irony, simplicity, the curious and the interesting details around him. He noticed a woman drawing water, a widow at the treasury, a tax collector's prayer, a Pharisee's showy robe, a beggar at the gate, an exasperated judge, a sister distracted by too many things, a thief suffering alongside him. He used these experiences to show us glimpses of God in daily living and wove these experiences into stories and parables to show us God's kingdom. By his habit of intertwining the spiritual with the mundane, the Spirit became flesh dwelling among us.

God is in it all. If we notice. And if we tell one another. God is in storm and tempest, in bold laughter and giggling children, in concert hall and airport lounge, in snow-white birds and lost change, and in the still small voice within us that is discernable only in silence, grief, and serenity. As Paul Tillich wrote, "Here and there in the world and now and then in ourselves is a New Creation."* God works on us, reaches out to us, makes himself known.

This book can be used personally for daily devotions and readings, as a month's reminders not to neglect the interior life. Read it individually. Or read it with friends, colleagues, family members, or fellow Christians, all reading the same stories on the same days in the same sequence. If you use it personally, don't sidestep the questions

9

at the end of each story. Mull the questions over, pray your way through them, ponder them in your heart, answer them for yourself, wrestle with them before God.

If you are part of a study or support group, an ongoing class or short-term gathering, a house group or adult Sunday school class, then take six weeks, one section per week, and agree together to each read the five stories for the week at home. Bring your thoughts or notes with you to the weekly gathering to share and discuss and learn and pray together for each other. If you have friends far away with whom you desire to further your walk with Christ, then covenant together to read the same essay each day, reflect on the questions, and then share your insights online each day. Learn from one another. Encourage one another. Rediscover grace together. Let the stories weave us together in Christ.

I pray this collection of stories serves to encourage and provoke us deeper into the spiritual life and nudge us forward in our following of Christ. I hope these stories help us realize that God is not an abstract philosophical principle, something way up there somewhere beyond our reach, but is a real and active presence in our lives. Threads of grace stream through each day connecting us to God and to one another.

Robert Schnase

---

* *The New Being* (Scribners, 1955); p. 18.

1

LOOKING WITHIN

THE BALANCING ACT

1

*Jesus said, "Come to me. Get away with me and you'll
recover your life. I'll show you how to take a real rest.
Walk with me and work with me—watch how I do it.
Learn the unforced rhythms of grace."*
(Matthew 11:28-29, *THE MESSAGE*)

I'm a rather eccentric journal keeper. I jot down daily notes into
a cheap notebook, recording observations, experiences, thoughts, and
feelings. Each year, I choose a few things in particular to count and
track, and I keep up with these in lists at the back of the journal.
Sometimes the numbers are humorous and playful, and other times
they are revealing and scary. For instance, during the twelve months
of last year, I ran or walked 1,132 miles for exercise, down from
1,514 the previous year. I read fourteen fewer books than in the year
before, and I gained thirteen pounds over the course of twelve
months. Nights spent in hotels went up by more than twenty. The
number of U.S. bird species I identified and recorded fell from 382
in the previous year to 253 last year!

If you take these numbers and project them forward for years to
come at the same rate, then I will stop seeing any birds at all in two
more years; I will read no books in 2012 and thereafter; I will stop
walking and running altogether within four years; by the end of the
next decade I'll live in a hotel full time, and I'll retire weighing 478

pounds! One of the reasons I pay attention to the numbers is to notice the trends and redress the imbalances.

We all wish we could live a totally balanced life—the perfect mix of family, personal, work, play, spiritual sustenance, reading, productivity, and health. If we could just get it right, then everything would work out well, and we'd live happily and fruitfully without much effort. But rather than having a totally balanced life, the best we can do is commit ourselves to the hard work of balancing, of constantly noticing and adjusting to keep from leaning too far one way or the other and falling into disaster.

The phrase "the balancing act" is a metaphor derived from the actual circus performances of days gone by. Remember the tightrope walker? She steps out onto a wire line stretched tightly high above the ground between two tall posts while carrying a long, horizontal pole. Inch by inch the tightrope artist gracefully moves across the wire. But whether she dances, walks, or stands still, there's always a constant perceptible motion of teetering slightly this way and that. These movements represent the inevitable pull of gravity to one side and then the other, and of her constantly offsetting these forces with tiny corrections and adjustments. The long, horizontal balancing pole totters slightly, rising a little on one side while falling a little on the other, and it does so from the first step until last. In short, the tightrope walker with her excellent sense of balance is never completely balanced; she is always balancing.

It has taken me a while to abandon the notion of a balanced life and to embrace the idea of balancing life. This difference may seem subtle, but is really quite significant. We are never the perfect weight; we never find the perfect mix of work and play; and we never manage to feed all our physical, emotional, and spiritual hungers with the exact portions necessary while also sustaining those around us and meeting all our professional and community obligations. We never find the ideal pattern that needs no reconsideration, recalibration, or rebalancing. Life is constant movement, forward stepping, sidetracking, detouring, self-correcting, getting a little lost, and finding our way back with the help of friends.

Balancing life's tasks, challenges, and callings is spiritual work, a matter of will, effort, prayer, decision, priority, change, growth, risk, grace, more grace, and reliance upon God and upon friends. Balancing all the stuff around us begins with balancing what's inside us. In our interior life, our life with God, we map the course, get the priorities right, open ourselves to the promptings of spirit, and remember who we are. Balancing is hard, but it's worth the effort. It keeps us from falling. It makes it possible to step forward without so much tension and worry. With practice, we may even begin to carry ourselves as gracefully forward as the woman on the wire does, even if we teeter and totter a little here and there.

Jesus' teachings are full of action words and heavy-loaded with imperatives: "Go . . . Teach . . . Heal . . . Baptize . . . Take up . . . Arise . . . Give . . . Tell . . ." His practice of ministry also included rich times of personal prayer, extended rest, time away, dinners with friends, long walks, fishing trips, stopovers at water wells, time in the Temple, sabbath. If Jesus' life required constant balancing, what makes us think we can work ours out with complete and un-improvable success?

How are you doing with your balancing act? What will you be like if all the patterns now so evident in your daily life continue uninterrupted into the future? Will you and I see fewer birds this year than last? Or will we notice more?

Questions

- What are two or three of the competing pressures, priorities, or desires that come to mind for you when you think about "the balancing act"?
- What practices or activities, friends and confidants, bring you back to yourself and restore a sense of proper proportion?
- Was there a time when things fell badly out of balance, and what helped you back?

Prayer

God, help me to follow you without falling; and when I fall, help me take the hand you offer. Amen.

LABYRINTH

2

*Thomas said to him, "How can we know the way?" Jesus
said to him, "I am the way, and the truth, and the life."*
(John 14:5-6)

While staying at a retreat center, I took a morning hike with my
binoculars in hand to search for birds. Along the path, I came to an
outdoor worship area and a large, rock-lined labyrinth. I've seen
labyrinths before at conference gatherings, clergy retreats, and spiritual formation events; and I must confess that I've never felt attracted
to the idea of walking a prescribed pathway, stopping to meditate at
key places according to printed guidelines, etc. I've had friends try
to push me into trying labyrinths, generating greater resistance from
me rather than provoking greater interest.

So here I was outdoors, alone under the hot sun on a beautiful
Texas hillside, far from anyone trying to talk me into anything; and
I found myself looking at the pathways through the labyrinth and
wondering why people find this helpful in their faith journeys. I
looked around to see if anyone could see me, and like someone
sneaking some hidden pleasure, I stepped toward the opening path at
the forward portion of the stone-lined labyrinth. And I started to walk
the dirt pathway.

I had not taken ten steps when a green-and-black-striped lizard darted down the pathway ahead of me and into the rocks. I stopped, and a flood of memories poured over me. I grew up in West Texas chasing these kinds of lizards. We called them "racers," and we saw them everywhere—along the streets as we walked to school, down the draw in back of our house when we would build forts of mesquite and rock, and along the dirt roads as we rode our bikes. I thought of childhood friends I hadn't seen in more than forty years and hadn't thought of for decades, and wondered where they were now and what pathways they'd taken through the years. Where are Jimmy and Mickey and Debbie and Eric and the people with the chickens next door and the woman who'd stand barefoot in her house robe and shoot rabbits invading her garden out her back door? I thought of all the horny toads we caught, and the turtles we raised, the snakes we saw, and all those "racers" that eluded us by their speed. Wow. It was a moment of simple refreshment.

I took a few more steps and came to a big turn and followed the path around. For some reason, this stirred my thinking about "big turns" in my early life—when our family moved from one town to another when I was in the third grade, when my brother went off to college, when I decided to leave behind my interest in math and science to pursue a liberal arts education. Some turns I made by choice; some were shaped by circumstances bigger than I. Some were good turns, and some I remember with a tinge of regret.

As I walked a few more steps, I came to a pile of rocks, neatly and carefully stacked high—a marker, a memorial, an Ebenezer (to use an ancient biblical term). These usually mark sacred places to memorialize holy moments, moments of transcendence and help and calling, and I wondered what experience stood behind the gathering of these stones before me. My own mind turned to the notion of calling, and I began to think about my own call, and all the places that were the "holy ground" of my own faith journey.

I felt the need to take off my shoes at this point on the pathway . . . something biblical there, about standing in the presence of the holy. Again, I looked to see that no one was around, slipped out of my running shoes, and carried them far down the path.

The thoughts about my own call to ministry and the special places along my journey also set my soul awash in memories of exceptional people—the pastors, the laity, the youth ministers and sponsors, and the Sunday school teachers. Each moved me along a path that had many and infinite choices going forward but in retrospect, each experience stands absolutely essential in forming who I am today. How could any of us get from there to here without the help of a thousand friends and strangers? God calls us through people, teaches us through people, leads us and sustains us through people. The most concrete and personal way God reaches down into our lives to work for our behalf is through people.

By now I was beginning to think maybe the hot Texas sun was boiling my brain to madness. How had this simple dirt and rock path in concentric loops elicited such unexpected memories and thoughts? I continued until I came to the center of the labyrinth. At the center there was a large gathering of rocks and sticks into a pile, and I conjectured that many people who had walked the labyrinth had done so carrying stones and then set them here, offering them up and relieving their burdens with the symbolic opening of their fists and letting go. Also on the center pile there were pieces of jewelry and coins and 12-step medallions and other little personal items. As I thought of what these people had offered, let go of, cast off, or sacrificed at this site, I became all the more moved to prayer. I was now sitting on the ground, cross-legged, shoeless, in blue jeans and baseball cap in the hot Texas sun, praying and letting go, letting go, letting go . . .

After a while I put on my shoes, stood up, gathered my binoculars, and prepared to leave. For the darnedest reason, I couldn't just walk straight out, although nothing barred my way. Instead, I retraced my steps through the entire labyrinth and left by the way I entered, but somehow refreshed, renewed, refocused.

Sometimes God uses the most ordinary means to take us to the most extraordinary of places. The simple rock pathways of a Texas Hill Country labyrinth became a reminder to me of the extraordinary journey of faith I have been privileged to take, and of all the unique pathways by which people come to the one who said, "I am the way, and the truth, and the life."

Questions

- What three "big turns" have you made that have brought you to who you are? How do you integrate those turning point events you regret into your story alongside those you celebrate?
- Who have been the people most instrumental in forming you and weaving into you the fabric of faith? How do you give them thanks, and give God thanks for them?

Prayer

Lord, help me accept the unchangeable past as a grace and to make of it a steppingstone toward a future full of life and hope.

THE CHAPEL ANGEL

3

*"I ask him to strengthen you by his Spirit—not a brute
strength but a glorious inner strength—that Christ will live
in you as you open the door and invite him in."*
(Ephesians 3:16-17, *THE MESSAGE*)

One evening while attending meetings at a university, I took an
evening walk by myself and slipped into the campus chapel. I felt
wonderfully fortunate to discover an excellent *a cappella* choir rehearsing in the chancel, and so I settled into a pew at the back. Im-
mersed in the music, I felt myself opening to a time of prayer.

As the peace of the moment deepened, I noticed a woman moving from pew to pew, straightening hymnals, picking up bits of paper,
placing envelopes in slots. She was one of the keepers of the chapel,
and eventually she made her way to where I was sitting. We began to
chat, and she asked what had brought me to campus and I told her
about the gathering of bishops. She seemed surprised, and asked if I
was a bishop. (I was in running shoes, jeans, and sweatshirt and
wasn't even wearing that little red lapel pin, so I guess I didn't look
very bishopy!)

After hearing that I was a bishop, she offered a thoughtful observation. She explained that she also helps with the upkeep of
Catholic chapel services, and she noticed that their Communion

liturgy is similar to that of the United Methodists. However, their liturgy always includes a prayer for the bishops and priests and servants of the church, and the United Methodist liturgy does not contain an explicit prayer for pastors. She suggested that this was a grave oversight, and that congregants and communicants should always be required to pray for their pastors. They should do it in every service, and they should do it joyfully and unselfishly because it's the right thing to do. And they should do it because, well, God knows pastors need prayer. She is United Methodist, and she wished the United Methodist liturgy included regular and frequent prayer for pastors.

I nodded and smiled at this unassuming messenger from God (also known as *an angel!*) sitting in the pew beside me. Now I knew what I was there to pray for. I was there in that chapel on that night to pray for my pastors.

Then she offered a further observation. She said that she did not think anyone should ever be allowed to complain about a pastor unless that person was also in constant prayer for the pastor. We should all desire our pastors to succeed, to fulfill their mission, to be strong and whole and healthy, and so we should pray for them, their families, their work, and their ministry. Imagine if every time we felt annoyed, discouraged, or disappointed by a pastor, we prayed for them with even greater eagerness and sincerity. Imagine if we felt as much or more an obligation to pray for a pastor as we feel to criticize or correct a pastor.

We visited a few more minutes, and then she left me to my own thoughts and prayers with the sweet music of the choir filling the chapel and touching my soul. And I began to pray for pastors—for pastors of my conference and beyond my conference, for United

Methodist pastors and those from other branches of the family tree, for those just starting out and those long since retired, for those enjoying every new day of engagement and for those feeling exhausted and weary, for those pastors who continue to surround us on earth and for those who cheer us on from the great cloud of witnesses in heaven.

Part of the great work and calling of being a pastor is how this grants us the rich privilege of praying for the people we serve, of finding ourselves on holy ground at hospital bedsides and family gravesides and at moments of personal conflict, reconciliation, change, and healing. We pray about things most people never realize we know about.

The keeper of the chapel reminded me that those who pray need our constant prayer as well. Prayer interweaves people into the fabric of the faith community. The threads of life are fragile, but the fabric of life and the strength of the community of faith are eternal. Prayer binds us to Christ and to one another. And pastors need our prayer as much as anyone else.

Give God thanks and praise for those who lead our congregations, for their lives and witness, their hard work and energetic vision, their deep commitment and high calling, their exhausting days and deep nights of the soul, their exultant moments and personal shortfalls, their outward focus and for the immeasurable impact they have on the lives of people and communities.

Pray for your pastor. Pray for your church. Pray for the community that your church and pastor has been called to transform. Pray for the world God has entrusted to us to serve.

23

Questions

- Why is praying for one another important for a group of Christ's followers?
- How do you pray for your pastor? Are your prayers conditional upon the pastor's performance, or unconditional and constant? Does your pastor know of your prayers?

Prayer

We offer to you in prayer, O God, our soul's sincere desire for the good of those who serve as well as for those served.

WHAT DOES IT MEAN?

4

"Jesus answered him, 'Very truly I tell you, no one can see
the kingdom of God without being born from above.' ...
Nicodemus said to him, 'How can these things be?'"
(John 3:3, 9)

I'm a birder, and I enjoy counting the hawks along the roadside as I drive from church to church and from speaking engagement to speaking engagement. In some areas of Missouri, I can count hundreds of Red-Tailed Hawks in a single day's drive, perched upright on tall trees and telephone posts overlooking fields and culverts for voles and mice. Occasionally, I see Red-Shouldered Hawks a little lower in the trees and farther back from the roadways, or Cooper's Hawks bulleting overhead.

Recently, while driving home from St. Louis in the cold gray rain, I noticed a bright patch of pure white in a tree where a Red-Tailed Hawk ought to be perched. It had the posture, shape, size, and behavior of a Red-Tailed Hawk; but this bird was completely white—not light, not Krider's Hawk beige, but white. I exited as soon as I could and returned back on the other side of the highway to get a closer look. The bird was a rare *albino* Red-Tailed Hawk.

In our science-oriented society, the first questions that come to mind are, "Where did it come from? What causes the color variation? How does it survive?"

But in the moment of awesome splendor, I couldn't help thinking of the way generations of Native Americans would look at the bird. The driving question would be, "What does it mean?" Often unusual sightings of birds or animals would portend something great or calamitous, and so the occasion would push a community into deep reflection, into the interior world of soul or the higher world of spirit and discernment.

This may seem a stretch, but this came to mind as I continued my drive home. It occurs to me that many of our most passionate church leaders and most fruitful congregations, when they are faced with unexpected events, focus on the same question. They give priority to "What does it mean?" over "What caused it?"

I served a congregation that developed a long-term downtown plan for ministry expansion, facility improvement, and property acquisition. The congregation committed itself to the plan and pursued it with diligence and effectiveness over several years. Then one day they received the devastating news that one of the property acquisitions that was central to their plan would never happen. Their long-term plan would never come to be. It was over. I suppose the church could have fallen into the trap of analyzing the questions to death, "How did this happen? What caused this?" They could have blamed and scapegoated or ignored and denied the significance of this reversal. They could still be arguing about it today, fourteen years later.

Instead, the church leaders gathered together a month after hearing the news, and one of the women on the committee courageously changed the focus. In effect, she asked, "What does this mean?" What does this mean for how we fulfill our mission, for how we reach young families, for how we become the church in this community for generations to come? Her emphasis was not on, "What caused this?"

but "Where does this lead us now? What will we become because of this? Where is God in this?" The committee's energy changed, and before the meeting was over, there were inspired ideas about a future different from what anyone had imagined. Five months later, after much consultation, discussion, and churchwide communication, the church voted overwhelmingly on a new plan, a new location, a new future.

Sometimes unexpected things happen in a church—a tragic fire, an unexpectedly large gift, changes in the neighborhood, a new zoning ordinance, the death of a key leader, the arrival of some new families. How a church responds while keeping a focus on its mission is critical.

The same is true in our personal lives. A devastating grief, an unanticipated layoff, an unplanned pregnancy, a windfall inheritance, a new twist in a relationship— any of these can become the occasion for looking back, blaming, overanalyzing, second-guessing, getting stuck. Or such events can mean the opening to a new chapter for our lives that we never imagined. In whatever circumstance we find ourselves, the most important decision is always the next one. And there is always a next one.

When the unexpected, unusual, and unplanned happens we cannot get bogged down only in the causes and reasons. There is also the spiritual question, "What does it mean? What does it mean for me, for us, for our community, for the life God has called me to and for the tasks God has entrusted to us?"

Okay. It was just an albino hawk, and . . . and an invitation to deeper reflection on the meaning of surprises in our lives.

Questions

- When did an unexpected event cause you to explore afresh your spiritual journey?
- "The most important decision is always the next one." What does that mean for you? How does this free you from the past and point you to the future?

Prayer

Lord, open us to the unexpected, to the new birth you intend for us, and to the new paths we have not planned, but which nevertheless lead us to you.

LOST COINS

5

"Or what woman having ten silver coins, if she loses one
of them, does not light a lamp, sweep the house, and
search carefully until she finds it?"
(Luke 15:8)

Our family recently returned from a couple of weeks of driving, meetings, driving, camping, driving, hiking, driving, visiting family, and driving some more. We covered over 3,000 miles, most of them in Texas.

But I'm happy to report that I'm fifty-two cents richer for the experience. That's how much money I found while running or walking for exercise in the mornings and evenings . . . three dimes, twenty two pennies, and one casino token! That brings the total to nearly six dollars I've found already this year.

I first started picking up change while training for the New York City Marathon in 1995. During the months of preparation, as I passed the miles along roadsides and sidewalks and parking lots, I'd always stop to pick up pennies, nickels, dimes, and quarters. I'd put them in a large jar, and that jar is now full to the top after eight marathons and more than a dozen years of running. I have found coins from Costa Rica, Germany, Mexico, Guatemala, Honduras, Canada, Korea, and South Africa as well as occasional dollar bills, and even the rare five and ten dollar bills. My biggest find was a twenty dollar bill! All of them are in the jar. Anytime I find a coin in the presence of my sons, one of us carries forth the family tradition that we started years ago by saying, "Well, I guess that makes it all worthwhile!"—a reference to the comment I used to make long ago after finishing 15-mile training runs only to pour out five pennies on the table when I returned. A lot of work for a little pay-off!

My favorite coins in the jar are those I picked up on the edge of destruction—those so badly scarred, scraped, bent, or chipped that a few more days of highway traffic and they would have been beyond recognition. Since I've had years of training at searching for lost coins, I occasionally impress friends with my ability to see, locate, and identify coins on concrete, even at long distances. Sometimes while running, I'll turn around, cross the street, and reach down to pick up a penny that barely caught my eye from the other side of the roadway. How do collectors see them when others don't? You see what you're looking for.

No preacher can talk about finding lost coins without somehow returning to the stories told by Jesus about lost things. In the fifteenth chapter of Luke, Jesus answers the religious "insiders"who are grumbling about his spending too much time with the "outsiders" by telling them three stories—about a lost sheep, a lost coin, and a lost son. How does the sheep get lost? It nibbles its way lost; through distraction, ignorance, naiveté, and simply following its own appetites without seeing the "big picture implications," the sheep ends up wandering away from the flock. How does the son get lost? Willful rebellion against his father—basically wishing his dad were dead so he could get all his dad's worldly possessions and do his own thing.

How does the coin get lost? It neither wanders nor rebels. It *gets* lost, *becomes* lost, *is* lost by someone else. No matter how you cut it, the lostness of the coin is described by a passive verb construction.

Someone loses it. Carelessness? Distraction? Apathy? Anger? Negligence? Accident? We don't know. But these attributes describe the person who loses it, not the coin itself.

Our congregations fulfill their mission in a sea of lost people, within and beyond our walls. There are so many ways we find ourselves cut off from God, from each other, from our families, from community, from our own best selves, from what God created us to be. We nibble ourselves lost, and we willfully rebel. The story of the ages is repeated in each of us.

But think about the people who aren't lost because of their own volition, but because we lose sight of them. Like throwaway coins on the side of the road, we drop them, lose them, let them slip through the cracks and out of view and out of mind. They aren't valuable enough for us to make the effort to find them.

Who are we losing sight of in our own churches? Older adults, people going through divorce who slip into inactivity, single moms who don't feel at home among us, families with children with special needs. And in our own communities? People get lost in our healthcare systems, our educational systems, our economic and political systems. Even our relatives become strangers to us. They disappear from our view right in our own everyday paths!

And we lose people around our own churches—people who live right in our own communities whom we cannot see. I was invited to meet with a congregation in South Texas, but I couldn't find a parking space near the church because of all the traffic from people attending a PTA meeting at the elementary school across the street from the church. As I met with the leaders, they said that their number-one concern was that there were no young people in their church or in their town anymore. When I told them I had to park a block away because of all the traffic at the elementary school across the street, the Anglo church leaders told me that I couldn't count those kids and young families—they're all Hispanic! The coin didn't ask to be lost, did it?

How did Jesus come up with this story of the lost coin? Surely people lost as many coins from their pockets and leather pouches in biblical times as we lose from our wallets and purses today. And I imagine that through his many miles of walking, Jesus must have occasionally reached down to pick up a lost coin and smile with his companions. Maybe he even kept a jar of lost coins himself, reminders of all the lost people he gathered around him to become his followers to transform the world he came to save. Maybe with each lost person he found, he said to himself, "That makes it all worthwhile!"

Questions

- Think about people you are at risk of losing touch with—relatives, neighbors, coworkers, church members. What restrains you from reaching out to them or taking initiative to renew relationships?
- When have you felt "lost," and who helped bring you back?

Prayer

Lord, starting today with one person, make me an instrument of your reconciling love. What I intend with my heart may I follow with my actions.

2
NOTICING GOD

STAYING AWAKE

6

"Beware, keep alert; for you do not know
when the time will come. . . . And what I say to you
I say to all: Keep awake."
(Mark 13:33-37)

Recently, I attended worship with my family, a rare occurrence since usually on Sundays, I'm on the road somewhere preaching or teaching. The Scripture was from Mark 13, including the mysterious, almost code-like apocalyptic images that baffle, provoke, irritate, electrify, terrify, or mystify so many readers. But there was one phrase that kept jumping out of the text, at once wonderfully simple as well as strikingly profound. In this one short and otherwise confusing text, Jesus repeats the simple imperative three times in quick succession: "Keep awake!"

For Jesus to repeat this so emphatically three times in a row implies that one of the great hazards of the faith journey is spiritual acquiescence, a kind of grogginess that dulls us to what is true, and truly important. Sleepiness of spirit means we miss out on what God is doing, and perhaps overlook the presence of Christ right in our midst. By simply falling asleep, spiritually speaking, we miss God and miss out on what God is calling us to be and do.

The peril of spiritual stupor is real, and we see this theme repeated in Scripture many times. The disciples who hiked to the mountaintop with Jesus almost missed the Transfiguration because they were sleepy! One story tells about someone whom others assumed was dead, but Jesus says, "He's not dead; he's sleeping." In the Garden of Gethsemane, on the night that the disciples knew would be Jesus' last among them, they fell asleep. Even after Jesus implored them to stay awake with him, they nodded off. Scripture also records one poor follower who dozed during a sermon and fell out the window. (Let that be a warning to the people in the pews!) If it hadn't been for Mary and company on Easter morning, the disciples would have slept through the resurrection of Christ. In my mind this also accounts for the person in need of healing who reported, "I see people as trees walking." A dulling of spiritual insight causes us to see people as things, and to overlook how each is a child of God made in the image of God.

Our twenty-year-old artificial Christmas tree crashed and died as we were putting it up last year. So in good Wesleyan form, "I submitted to be more vile" and headed to places I usually avoid during the Christmas rush in search of a tree. And "what to my wondering eyes did appear?" Tons of bleary-eyed, hurried people already looking overdone by the "joys" of the holiday season.

As I people-watched for a while, I thought about how easily people stop becoming people to us when we are hurried and bleary-eyed. People become things, objects, mechanisms in the machinery that bring to us the things we want, or obstacles and competitors to us acquiring what we want. The unseen laborers in the field who pick our fruit and the farmers who hire them; the machinists in the factories that manufacture our cars and the convenience store clerks we pay for the gas to drive them; the drivers who deliver our goods and the stockers who stack them on shelves for us; the clerks and waitresses and cooks and servers and tellers we encounter every day—and all the other people who stand in front of us and behind us at the check-out line, and all those who cut into traffic ahead of us on the roads and crunch popcorn behind us at movie theaters—if we're not careful, we become so distracted by things that do not matter, so driven by things that are of little account, or so tired and burned out and spiritually exhausted, that they stop being human to us. We lose sight of people, of purpose, of what matters most. "Keep awake," Jesus says. "Be alert." "Stay attentive!" Following Christ, staying awake with him, requires a constant spiritual acuity, an attentiveness, a preparedness of soul and character, a kind of spiritual attention. Jesus says, "I was a stranger and you came to me. . . . I was hungry and you gave me something to eat." Do we notice him? Stay awake.

The practice of attentiveness involves noticing what God notices and seeing the world through God's eyes. It takes a passionate attentiveness rather than a groggy indifference to notice the movement of the Spirit, to hear whispers of God's grace, to discern the presence and power of God among us, to identify the calling of God. It takes discipline and an intentional practicing of attentiveness for us to develop the interior life, the life of the Spirit, the life of love, grace, forgiveness, mercy, justice, hope.

As we practice spiritual attentiveness, we begin to see the world differently. We stay awake; we become alive; we practice resurrection. Through the eyes of faith, we fathom such questions as: Where is God in this? How have I seen God at work in the last few days? What might God be trying to alert me to? What does the world look like through God's eyes?

Jesus' teaching is wonderfully simple but profoundly important. "Stay awake!" Be alert. Notice. Notice people. Notice God at work. Look for the coming of Christ again and again into our lives and into the lives of others around us. Listen for God and God's calling. Stay awake!

Questions

- Who are the people you regularly see in your life without really seeing? Who are some people you see as "trees walking"?
- What does it feel like to be unseen by others right in front of us?
- What exercises or practices help you "keep awake" to the life of the Spirit, the presence of others, and the callings of God?

Prayer

Open the eyes of my eyes, Lord, to see you and your kingdom again and again as if for the first time.

PADDLE OR DIE!

7

"Keep your eyes on Jesus, who both began and finished
this race we're in. Study how he did it. Because he never
lost sight of where he was headed—that exhilarating finish
in and with God—he could put up with anything
along the way . . ."
(Hebrews 12:2, *THE MESSAGE*)

My son and I took a 15-mile bike ride on the Katy Trail that runs along the Missouri River near where we live. The river was swollen far beyond its usual banks because of flooding rains across the Midwest. In the middle of the wide river we could see a canoe being pushed along by the strong and steady flow, and the two canoeists were steadily paddling straight downstream.

Ever wonder why canoeists paddle while going downstream?

I've spent a lot of time canoeing and kayaking over the years, but I learned about currents, rapids, and whitewater in Central America. While studying Spanish in Costa Rica, my sons and I took a weekend break and joined a raft trip on the Pacuare River. The rapids were posted as Level Three as I recall, but the river there was swollen, too, and the ratings didn't match U.S. measurements. In short, once we got on the water it felt like we were heading over Niagara Falls, over and over again, hour after hour, frequently finding ourselves flung out of the raft and struggling for our lives in the deep and dangerous currents. I don't care to repeat the experience anytime soon. The T-shirt my boys bought afterward read, *"Remar o Morir*!" Paddle or Die!

But I did learn a few things. The guide sat at the back of the raft calling out instructions about which side to paddle on, and how intensely to do so. At critical junctures, he'd bark out, "Right!" "Hard Left!" "Stop!" "Back Right Hard!" as we approached boulders the size of buses and were slung through falls and shoots as high as houses. During one period of relative calm, as the river was propelling us down toward the next deathtrap, the guide was telling us to paddle gently on both sides. One of my sons asked him, "Why do we have to paddle when the river is pushing us downstream anyway?" He smiled and said, "The only way we have any control over the direction we are going is for us to be moving just a little faster than the current below us. So we have to always paddle, or else we just get pushed along out of control." If we want to navigate with purpose and to control our direction rather than becoming a victim to forces beyond our control, we have to keep paddling. "Remar o Morir!"

We live in a whitewater world. Things change so rapidly—communications systems, the makeup of our communities, the tastes and habits of new generations, the expectations and values of congregations, the competing claims of a secular society for our hearts and minds. This is true in our personal and family lives as well—the phases and steps of a marriage, the transitions of our children, the heartbreaks and hopes, deaths and births, losses and gains, brokenness and reconciliation. Unceasing motion. We live fast-forward lives.

Life is constantly pushing us along, and sometimes there seems little we can do; we feel like victims, vulnerable and powerless. But we can't stop paddling. We can't stop learning, growing, changing, adapting. It's by thinking and rethinking things, praying anew each day, by committing and recommitting to the right things, and by reimagining God's will for us that we are able to navigate through the white-water world. It's by depending upon friends, knowing the water, and practicing constantly that we remain strong. Life requires an agility of spirit, forward movement, effort, vision and a keen awareness of the forces at work around us and how to use them for the purposes of Christ rather than become overwhelmed by them.

The canoeists in the middle of the wide Missouri were running perfectly straight down the middle of the river, confidently and purposefully toward their goal, using the rush of the water to propel them, but paddling just enough to stay ahead of the flow so that they could control their direction. If they stopped paddling, even for a minute, the river would have turned them sideways, then over and under, according to the whims of the wild and never-ceasing current.

Keep paddling!

Questions
- What are the pressures and currents of your whitewater world?
- How do you keep paddling? How do you learn, adapt, grow, and change so the currents don't overwhelm and destroy you?

Prayer
Make me new each day, and give me imagination, strength, and friends, Lord, for the facing of this hour.

DO NOT ENTER ON SUNDAYS

8

*"Don't become so well-adjusted to your culture that you
fit into it without even thinking. Instead, fix your attention
on God. You'll be changed from the inside out."*
(Romans 12:2, *THE MESSAGE*)

I visited a church located in the downtown area of a small community. There are three or four churches on the same block, and it's hard to tell where one parking lot ends and the parking for the next church begins. To moderate the high volume of traffic caused by attendees from all the churches coming and going at the same time each Sunday morning, the city puts up temporary signs in the middle of the street to direct traffic to run one way. As I approached the church from the wrong way, I suddenly came upon the sign: "Do Not Enter on Sunday Before Noon."

I know that the people who placed the sign have good intentions, but you have to admit that it gives pause for reflection. The first thought that comes to mind is how many churches put up such "signs" like this without knowing it. A signboard with chipping paint and outdated information that's printed so small that it can only be read by pedestrians; a parking lot full of potholes; outside doors with no signage to give any indication where to enter; a dark, dirty, and smelly sanctuary; a nursery with unsafe fixtures, old paint, and musty odors—all these are just slightly more subtle ways of saying, "Stay Away," "Go Somewhere Else," "Do Not Enter on Sundays"!

Next, I thought of all the influences from our culture that tell people to stay away from church on Sunday morning. Our culture no longer supports church participation the way it did in the past.

Imagine that you were on a high school athletic team in the 1950's. The coach says, "I wish we could have one more practice before the big game next week." You raise your hand and say, "Coach, why don't we practice on Sunday morning?" What would the coach of the 1950's say to that?

The coach would say, "Are you crazy? You need to be in church on Sunday just like I'll be in church on Sunday, and just as the principal, the teachers, and the custodians of this school will be in their churches on Sunday!" In the 1950's, our whole culture supported church attendance. Stores and offices were closed, elementary and teen sports were suspended, television and entertainment options were limited, and there were no Internet, NFL games, NBA tournaments, fishing contests, or spelling bees on Sundays. The sign that culture lifted up said, "Enter Church on Sunday Mornings"!

Now, imagine that you are an elementary-age kid today on the community league soccer team. The big tournament is scheduled for Sunday morning, and you bravely raise your hand and tell your coach, "I can't play on Sunday because I have to be in church with my family."

What is the coach's response in 2009? "I'm sorry, but if you can't play on Sunday, then you're off the team." Culture today is like a giant vacuum cleaner sucking people out of the pews of our churches on Sunday mornings. Malls are open all day, coffee shops and restaurants fill up from early morning, carwashes do their best business, and communities host marathons, fairs, fundraisers, and tournaments without regard to church. The sign culture lifts up for churches today is "Do Not Enter on Sundays Before Noon."

In recognition of this changing reality, many churches innovate with creative meeting times and diverse meeting places to involve people in worship and study. They offer services in homes, in public places, in parks, hotels, and on practice fields. They offer ministries on Saturday mornings, Wednesday nights, Thursdays at midday. They adapt and change to reach others. They don't let the "Do Not Enter on Sundays Before Noon" thinking impede their ministry.

Following Christ today requires countering culture. Little in our society rewards or values the development of the interior life. Few elements of our commercial and materialist culture support generosity, service, or sabbath. Following Christ requires cutting against the current, swimming upstream. It means moving past the "Do Not Enter" sign when culture tries to make it all look like a one-way street.

Questions

- How do you make sure that your church is not unintentionally hanging a sign that reads: "Do Not Enter"?
- How do you confront or accommodate to the changing role of culture that offers so many conflicting choices for Sunday morning activities?
- How is following Christ countercultural?

Prayer

Help me fix my eyes upon you, Lord. Change me from the inside out.

NOTICING GOD

THE BEAR

9

"Your body has many parts—limbs, organs, cells—but
no matter how many parts you can name, you're still one
body. It's exactly the same with Christ. By means of
his one Spirit, we all said good-bye to our partial
and piecemeal lives."
(1 Corinthians 12.12-13, *THE MESSAGE*)

While hiking a mountain trail in Big Bend National Park (Texas) with my two sons, my eyes were scanning the treetops for birds when I saw some movement. My mind tried to comprehend what I was seeing as I focused on something large and black moving nearly twenty feet high in a tree, and no more than fifty feet from us. Was I seeing the back of a Turkey Vulture, a Black Hawk, a Zone Tailed Hawk? Then I realized that the dark, triangular shape was the face and forehead of a Black Bear! She was dining contentedly on some berries, acorns, or pines high up in the tree when she suddenly turned to look at us with the same curiosity with which we were looking at her. I made sure each of the boys had a good look and then we quietly and quickly continued down the trail. We began to notice all the "bear-warning" signposts we'd been walking by and overlooking before our encounter beside the path.

This is the second time we've seen Black Bear in West Texas; the first was a few years ago. Until fifteen years ago, Black Bear were unheard of in the area. They had not been seen for over fifty years. Now they are coming back, and sightings are not unusual. But for me, seeing them is always an awesome and humbling experience.

Remember the old story about the two buddies hiking in the woods when they came across a bear? The bear looked up at them, growled ferociously and got ready to pounce on them. Slowly, the first hiker began to take off his backpack and set it on the ground, then he took off his water bottle and his binoculars and set them down as well. His friend said to him, "Surely you don't think you can outrun a bear!" He answered, "I don't have to outrun a bear—I just have to outrun you!"

I love the way that joke captures the cynical, self-centered, individualist notions of the world: "As long as I get out alive, everything else is okay." That explains much about why we have the medical systems, the politics, and sometimes even the churches we have. "As long as my needs are taken care, as long as I experience no problems, as long as I make it, everything is fine."

We can do better.

After our encounter on the path, I've taken a keener interest in what you're really supposed to do in the presence of a bear if you come along one while hiking. A group should stay together so that they become a strong, highly visible, united entity. Bears don't like things bigger than themselves, and they'll move away. In other words, instead of hoping I can get out, regardless of the others and at the expense of the slowest, we should figure out how to work together. If one of us doesn't make it okay, then none of us has succeeded.

There are various bears on the prowl out there in our communities these days—economic reversals, repossessed homes, lay-offs. Drug use and alcoholism are hot on the heels of some of our youth. Divorce, loneliness, abuse, violence. And there are the spiritual beasts, the internal ones: the lion of despair crouches at the door and the bear of cynicism stands ready to feast on us. The daily grinding down of spirit and hope, the churning and churning that seem to take us no where—these can eat us alive. And much of the self-help literature proposes "me-first" success models. I've succeeded if I survive, regardless of what happens to you. As the hiker in the story says, "I just have to outrun you!"

The way of Christ dares to propose that our lives are interconnected. We're part of the body, and one part cannot say to another, "I have no need for you." The gift of community means I am in you and you are in me because we are both in Christ. We pray for one another, walk with one another, learn from one another, work with one another, encourage one another; and by seeing ourselves as connected to one another in Christ, we come into the fullness of what God created us to be. Following Christ is never a solitary affair.

That's why Jesus sent the disciples out "in pairs" or "two by two." The better to scare away the bears!

Questions

- Where do you see the me-first thinking at work in your life? Your church? Your community?
- What obligation do we have to protect other people's children from drugs, or to help those who cannot pay to receive medical care? Is it each of us alone, or is there another way?

Prayer

Rescue me, Lord, from thinking I can do it all by myself. Rescue me from thinking that threats to others are no threat to me or to your kingdom.

IT'S WORTH IT!

10

"God looked over everything he had made;
it was so good, so very good!"
(Genesis 1:31, *THE MESSAGE*)

I'm sitting in a university concert hall as I write this. My teenage son is rehearsing *Carmina Burana* with a several-hundred member choir. Since I will miss the actual performance because I'll be out of town, I've been attending the rehearsals with him. The music is powerful, the singers outstanding, and the university choir director fantastic.

A few minutes ago, the director focused the attention of the choir on a particular section of the music. He had them repeat, and repeat again, a particularly difficult phrase, taking special care to break down the pronunciation of the Latin. He wrote the words out on a chalkboard, pointing out how one word ends in *m*, and the next starts with *st*, and how the choir had to be sure that the *m*, *s*, and *t* sounds are all heard, even though the phrase moves quickly. He had the choir take it syllable by syllable, words only, and then measure by measure, music only, and then put it all together.

At one point he said, "I know it's tedious to go over this much detail, but it's worth it." Then he became passionately emphatic, drawing everyone up straight in their seats, as he continued, "It's worth it

51

to get it just right . . . it's like the color in a painting; it just wouldn't look the same or be as effective if you just settle for whatever you splash up there first. It's the same with pronunciation in music. The art requires that we get it just right. It's the difference between mediocrity and excellence. The artist made the effort, and so should we. The composer made the effort, and so should we. It's worth it. It's always worth it!"

Imagine if that spirit and value permeated our worship services, the music of the services, our children's ministries, our mission projects, our facilities, our publications, the quality of our pastoral care, and our passion for the people who live in our communities. Imagine if that striving for excellence marked our personal efforts at following Christ, the quality of our service to others in need, our desire to offer our utmost and highest.

God created the heavens and the earth, and called them what? So so? OK? God saw everything he had made and it was *very good*!

Paul wrote, "And I will show you a still more . . . " Mediocre way? No. "I will show you a still more *excellent* way" (1 Corinthians 12:31).

Imagine if in our serving and singing, in our teaching and preaching, in our helping and giving, we carried with us the spirit of "Our Creator made the effort to make things just right, and so should we. It's worth it!"

I recall the leader of a Volunteers-in-Mission team who was training us as we prepared to spend several days doing construction work on the houses of families living in extreme poverty. Some of us would be replacing roofs and others would be building wheelchair ramps. Some would be painting walls and others replacing floors. At one point in the training, he said, "You may be tempted to think that even if you do a sloppy job, that's OK since the house will still be better than it was before you got here." Then his voice cracked with emotion as he said, "But that's not good enough. You should work on this like you're working on your own mother's house. This should be the best job you have ever done. These people are worthy of Christ's sacrifice, and they are worthy of our best efforts."

None of us are perfect, and I'm not suggesting we revert to a works righteousness that has us trying to earn God's love by our efforts. But our passionate love for God and neighbor should draw out of us a taste for excellence, a desire to offer our utmost and highest. Layperson or pastor, paid or volunteer, young or old—the service and leadership we offer should be our best. We received God's greatest offering in Jesus Christ. We cannot help but offer our best in return.

Questions

- When have you found yourself offering less than your best in serving others in Christ's name?
- What does excellence in serving, in giving, in singing, in leading, in caring mean?

Prayer

You have offered to us the ultimate and perfect gift of your Son, dear God. Help us to excel in all things good, to your great glory.

FINDING COURAGE

3

DO NOT BE AFRAID

11

*"She was thoroughly shaken. . . . But the angel
assured her, 'Mary, you have nothing to fear.
God has a surprise for you.' "*
(Luke 1:29-30, *THE MESSAGE*)

I heard a brief devotion focused on Luke 1:26-38, the scene where the angels foretell the birth of Jesus to Mary. The pastor humorously reminded us that in Scripture, whenever you hear the words, "Be not afraid," then watch out! Something huge is about to happen. Hold on to your seats because the world is about to turn upside down!

Mary receives that word from the angels, and she finds herself "perplexed"; Joseph receives a similar word and begins to sort through what it means to be engaged to a woman bearing a child; the shepherds in the field are given the message and they seem genuinely awestruck by the possibilities. This heavenly imperative is repeated in choruses throughout Scripture, including at Jesus' tomb on the first Easter morning and when Jesus calms the storm.

"Do not be afraid" always accompanies an event that totally changes how we see and experience the world a miraculous birth, God taking human form, life that is unrestrained by death, a miracle. In each case, the phrase introduces a revealing of God that brings great hope. But for us to receive the hope, the angels always feel the need to relieve our fears.

This leads to some reflection about how hopes and fears intertwine. It's no accident that the hymn reads, "The hopes and fears of all the years are met in thee tonight." Times of great fear and anxiety send us searching for hope, struggling to discern it, and reaching to grasp it.

The opposite is also true: Times of great hope stir up our fears. Even positive changes are disruptive and disturbing and painful. They are wrought with risk, loss, challenge, and threat. Hope and growth and change and uncertainty are both a wonderful and a wonderfully stressful mix.

We cannot grab on to something new without letting go of something old. We don't fear change as much as we fear loss.

Nothing so deeply captures the interweaving of our hopes and fears as the birth of a baby. I remember the moment more than twenty years ago when I was handed my son to hold in my arms less than fifteen minutes after his birth. My soul was overwhelmed with awe, joy, and hope. I sat down in a rocker and couldn't take my eyes off him. His little fingers looked exactly like mine! Few moments in life have so deeply moved me. But also with his birth and his becoming part of our lives, a whole new host of fears were born, the natural anxieties that come with the awesome responsibility of parenting. That mixture of hopes and fears continues to this day, and probably will as long as I have my breath. Anyone with responsibility and hope needs the angel's reminder, "Do not be afraid."

In a book for church leaders, the author describes stress as a necessary element of change. Too much stress or purposeless stress depletes and distracts even the best of disciples. But the complete absence of stress can indicate a lack of passion, a loss of purpose, a shortage of commitment, an absence of vision. Without stress there may be no fear, but there is also no hope.

Those who feel prompted by the Holy Spirit to bold new service and creative new ministry and passionate new outreach always step out into uncertain places as they seek to follow Christ and serve others.

That's why we need the messages from the angels. In uncertain and turbulent times, we need the assurance of hope. Also in the times of great hope and passion, we need the reminder, "Do not be afraid."

Move forward. Step bravely. Follow Christ. Encourage one another. "Do not be afraid."

Questions
- Why does even positive change cause us to fear?
- Who brings the angel's message, "Do not be afraid," to you?

Prayer

May anxious thoughts and worrisome feelings not rob me of the assurance of your presence, Lord, nor of the will to step forward in your name.

FINDING COURAGE

THE RECKLESSNESS OF FAITH

12

*"By an act of faith, Abraham said yes to God's call
to an unknown place. . . . When he left he had no idea
where he was going."*
(Hebrews 11:8, *THE MESSAGE*)

William Sloane Coffin wrote, "I love the recklessness of faith.
First you leap, and then you grow wings."*

At first hearing, this appealingly poetic clip evokes a smile. Upon
deeper reflection, I'm touched by its penetrating truthfulness.

Faith is reckless. According to the Letter to Hebrews, Abraham
set out not knowing where he was going. This doesn't sound well
thought out. It's unsafe, edgy, impulsive, dangerous. And yet, he and
Sarah are lifted up as models of faith!

Every meaningful endeavor requires stepping into uncertainty,
doesn't it? Getting married, having children, responding to the call to
follow Christ, offering oneself to ministry, initiating a new outreach to
the poor . . . these are all things we might think differently about if we
fully understood all their implications, and all the places these decisions might take us that we would never go on our own. It's reckless
to think we can start a church, build a youth program, change our worship style, offer a stranger an invitation, make a difference through our
service. It's reckless to send our money overseas to build churches and
schools in faraway places that may be destroyed by the next flood or

overrun by the next invasion. It's reckless to invite young people with little or no faith background into our churches and let them help shape our ministries.

Then Coffin describes the recklessness of faith this way: "First you leap, and then you grow wings."

When we step out in faith, not knowing where we are going, we discover that we are not alone. We are unexpectedly sustained in ways we could never imagine. Step by step, we move forward into the fog, usually with just enough light to see the next inch. As Scripture says, we go "from strength to strength." We discover that where there was no hope before, there is now new possibility. We find that there are enough resources, prayers, people, and spiritual sustenance in each day to make it through that day. We discover courage inside ourselves we never realized was possible. We discover colleagues, peers, mentors, and fellow travelers and coworkers that we never imagined existed. We find wings, wings we didn't know were possible until we took the leap.

My favorite line is the first: "I *love* the recklessness of faith." The writer stands in awe at the pattern of risky, forward-leaning steps that are repeated over and over in lives, ministries, and churches around the world. Rather than feeling fearful or upset at the peril of risky faith ventures, the writer embraces it. Forward movement toward God involves a reasonable and predictable riskiness, and that's all right. Following Christ is a wonderfully and dangerously risky undertaking, and that's all right. Finding the inner courage to leap is one of the graces of life.

I enjoy the privilege of visiting many "reckless" congregations. It's reckless for a congregation to offer edgy worship in addition to a traditional service, but by doing so it reaches many young people that other churches miss. It's risky for a church to build an expansive new extension for children in a lightly populated rural area, and yet the church is overflowing with new families. It's reckless for a congregation to give birth to a new separate congregation, but by doing so, it reaches a different generation. It's reckless for a congregation in financially stressful times to commit to a larger investment in overseas mission, but I know one who is thriving by doing so. I love the recklessness of these congregations. I love the recklessness of faith.

The adjectives of the Five Practices—*radical, passionate, intentional, risk-taking,* and *extravagant*—are all dangerously edgy. They push us into areas of uncertainty and discomfort. These words cause us to ask questions about whether we are playing it too safe and too comfortable. They pull us forward toward new creativity, and they pull us out of ourselves into the lives and communities around us. They help us risk. They help us embrace the recklessness of faith.

The adjectives resonate with our calling because Jesus' ministry was radical, passionate, intentional, risk-taking, and extravagant. Jesus understood the recklessness of faith. First, you leap. Then you grow wings.

Questions

- What is "reckless" about faith?
- What have you done in response to the prompting of God's Spirit that you never imagined you would do?

Prayer

Give me courage please, Lord. Give me a heart strong enough to cause me to act in your service, even when I haven't figured out all the answers and implications.

---

* *Credo* (Westminster John Knox, 2005); p. 7.

FINDING COURAGE

DON'T LET WORRY WIN

13

*"For during a severe ordeal of affliction, their abundant
joy and their extreme poverty have overflowed in a wealth
of generosity on their part."*
(2 Corinthians 8:2)

Over the years, I have learned that I usually make my biggest
mistakes when I'm tired. When I don't attend to patterns of rest,
sleep, exercise, and time away, and just keep grinding away at work
day after day, I become more likely to say things I wish I could take
back, make decisions that aren't constructive, and foster an atmos-
phere that isn't conducive to anyone's best attitude and fruitfulness.

I think many individuals and organizations make their biggest
mistakes when they allow fear, anxiety, and worry to influence their
decisions. Gripped by fear, we tend to lose focus and forget purpose.
If we're not careful, community and trust become brittle, tempers in-
tensify, and we move into a reactive mode rather than a thoughtful
and intentional form of deliberation.

When people of faith react in fear, the decisions are likely for
short-term outcomes. Fear stifles creativity, and when people of
prayer and spiritual depth respond in reactive ways, they limit alter-
natives and possibilities that they might ordinarily consider in less
stressful times. Fear closes the door to the Spirit's wisdom.

Perhaps that is why so many Scriptural passages repeat a common refrain, "Do not be afraid." That's what the angel said to Mary at the Annunciation, what the heralds of Christ's coming told the shepherds in the field, what Jesus said to the disciples on the stormy sea, and what the risen Christ said to the women at the tomb. That's the message the disciples, huddled together in fear after the death of Jesus, had trouble hearing. "Have no fear" does not mean we avoid legitimate concern and engagement. It means, "Don't let worry win." When worry wins, we lose. When worry wins, the purpose and ministry of Christ gets hijacked, derailed, ignored, and avoided. Don't let worry win.

Like everyone else, I've cringed each evening during recent months to hear of the downward spiral of the financial markets. I think of people losing jobs, closing businesses, anxious about their houses, fearful for their retirements, wondering about their college savings funds. I think of the churches we serve and their pledge campaigns, their budgeting for ministry, the missions they support, the ministries they offer, the building projects that are underway. I think this season requires of us a special steadiness of hand. Don't rush to make permanent decisions based on temporary setbacks. We don't know how long and how deep this troubling time may last. We will know much more as the months unfold. Make prudent decisions rather than panicked ones. When gripped by fear, sometimes we feel we must act, that we must do something. Doing something gives us a sense of control. This has caused countless people to sell stocks at incredible losses, leaving investments that will one day rebound. Check the motivation . . . fear or faith? Reactive or purpose-driven? Impulsively or deliberately and prayerfully considered?

Someone once told me, "The person with the fullest cup requires the steadiest hand." For those of us with responsibilities for our families, for our churches, for our communities, or for employees: now is not the time to let worry win

In our congregational life, we do well to keep the focus on the purpose of our ministries, even and especially during stressful times. Challenging times do not relieve us of the joyful obligation of worshipping God with glad and generous hearts; of serving others with compassion, mercy, and justice; of studying God's Word and teaching the children; and of inviting others into Christ. Challenging times do not relieve congregations, or the individuals who comprise them, of the calling to be generous and giving.

Many of the ministries that our congregations support—relief and assistance ministries, women's shelters, feeding and homebuilding ministries, ministries that help children and the poor, scholarship programs—are seeing their expenses increase even as the need for their services intensifies. They need us more now than ever.

The element of character and soul we call generosity is not seasonal, temporary, or only for smooth and easy times. Rather, generosity is our way of being in the world as followers of Christ because it's the way God works in the world. As Paul writes of the church of Macedonia, "for during a severe ordeal of affliction, their abundant joy and their extreme poverty have overflowed in a wealth of generosity on their part. For, as I can testify, they voluntarily gave according to their means, and even beyond their means, begging us earnestly for the privileges of sharing in this ministry" (2 Corinthians 8:2-4). Struggling against conditions we can hardly imagine, these early Christians did not let worry win. In our following of Christ, may we learn from them.

FINDING COURAGE

Questions

- Exhaustion, anxiety, anger, loneliness—what conditions most hamper your ability to make good and clear decisions? How do you keep self-aware of their influence?
- What causes you to lose sleep?
- What helps you keep proportional and appropriate concern from becoming a destructive and distracting anxiety? What helps you keep worry from winning?

Prayer

In my moments of panic, Lord, help me breathe—just breathe—until sustained by your Spirit, I discover the peace you give, a peace the world cannot take away.

PLEASE, LORD, SEND SOMEONE ELSE

14

"O my Lord, please send someone else."
(Exodus 4:13)

I was rereading the account of God calling Moses to return to Egypt to set free the people of Israel. The text says God hears the cries of the people and knows their sufferings. And then God puts the question to Moses of going to work on God's behalf, and Moses offers several good excuses: "Why me?" "They won't listen to me." "I'm not any good at public speaking." The line that I've probably read a thousand times, but never really focused on is this: "O my Lord, please send someone else" (Exodus 4:13). You can't get any more explicit than that; and Moses' plea before God expresses complete exasperation, fear, and near despair at the overwhelming task ahead that God is calling him to do. After Moses gets into the task and makes his first few attempts without success, you can detect the utter sense of failure when he says to God, "Why did you ever send me?" (Exodus 5:22). Ever felt that way?

Every single significant endeavor that God has ever called us to undertake has begun with a bucket load of excuses, justifications, and attempts to avoid the task. A regular and predictable part of responding to God's call (in little daily things and big audacious projects) is overcoming the sense that we are ill-equipped, unprepared, ineligible, unworthy, too old, too young, too inexperienced, not strong enough, not courageous enough, not faithful enough, or not smart enough to meet the overwhelming need and challenge. And while we have a thousand ways of wording it, we basically want to say, "O my Lord, please send someone else." And even after we get into the task, we slip back into, "Why did you ever send me?"

Any mission and outreach initiative, the start of any effective ministry, the genesis of any social change, the founding of every congregation we now serve—all required the gifts of women and men who doubted, questioned, resisted, and tried to avoid the task by saying, "O my Lord, please send someone else." But they also had enough faith and trust to open themselves to let God's Spirit work through them despite the insecurities and self-doubts. They feared and fought and avoided and denied, but in the end, they said, "Yes. Here I am. Send me. Use me, Lord."

These passages from Hebrew scripture resonate with the powerful scene in the Garden of Gethsemane. Jesus, in the moment that pierces through any shallow or naive notions we might have about the call of God, says, "Now my soul is troubled. And what should I say—'Father, save me from this hour'? No, it is for this reason that I have come to this hour" (John 12:27).

Early in my ministry, I was called at 4 A.M. to go to the hospital. A couple I knew closely as friends and church members had unexpectedly lost their child in the middle of the night. The drive to the hospital that morning was longer and darker and more forbidding than any I've ever taken. What would I say? What would I do? Nothing in any of my training and nothing in my experience or natural intuitions gave me a sense of confidence. I felt totally inadequate to the task and not at all sure what the task would require. "O my Lord, please send someone else."

As I parked the car and moved toward the emergency room entrance, I stopped and prayed. The passage from Gethsemane came to mind in that moment. In my own words, I found myself sighing, "What do I say, Lord? Take this away? Get me out of here? Save me from this hour? No. This is the reason you have sent me. This is why I am here. I don't know what I'm going to say or what I'm going to do, but I trust that you have brought me here for a purpose. I'm here for you." I walked into the room where my friends stood, and we fell into a profound and lasting embrace, weeping together. Every step and every action and every word from there came one at a time in its proper time. The Lord provided.

The occasion of my revisiting this Scripture has been some reflection on one of the Five Practices—Risk-Taking Mission and Service. Part of the risk is that we might surrender to the resistances, that we might let our own fears and excuses win the day, and that we could miss out on what God has planned for us in God's calling of us. The next time we hear ourselves say, "O my Lord, please send someone else," I hope we remember to stop, listen, pray, breathe, and then think about what God may be offering.

Questions

- When have you recently said, "Lord, please send someone else"?
- What's the best excuse you use to avoid doing something you feel God may be prompting you to do?
- How have you learned to overcome internal resistances to do something purposeful for Christ?

Prayer

For those moments today when we have been what you have called and created us to be, we give you thanks, O Lord.

An Invincible Summer

15

*"The resurrection life you received from God is not a
timid, grave-tending life. It's adventurously expectant,
greeting God with a childlike 'What's next, Papa?' "*
(Romans 8:15, *THE MESSAGE*)

Last week, a huge ice storm hit the southern half of our state with
devastating effect. For the last couple of days, I've been reading
emails from pastors and relief workers about households without
electricity, the closing of schools and churches, the irreplaccable loss
of ancient trees, the extraordinary damage to homes and businesses.
During the last few weeks, I've awakened to temperatures as low as
eight and five and two degrees, and even minus two degrees. Like
everyone else, I've trudged through snow, slid on ice, and tried to
disguise the worry in my voice as I've sent my son off each day for
his fifty mile drive to school and back. Winter has been real this year.
Really real.

I'm a South Texas boy. I grew up in desert terrain. It snowed once
when I was in the third grade, and that only lasted a day. We called
off school for days! During the twenty years before moving to Missouri, I lived where there are parrots in palm trees during the winter,
and where freezes are measured by the number of hours the temper-
ature dips below thirty-two rather than by weeks without rising above
thirty-two.

Maybe it's because of my desert upbringing and Texas blood that I need outdoors and sunlight, and my soul feels constricted when I'm forced inside for too long. All my favorite pastimes draw me outside—running, walking, birding, hiking, canoeing, kayaking, fishing, camping. I need outside time in each day. I need sun on my face.

This past Saturday, the weather broke and the sun came shining through. It was like an unexpected reprieve, a precious grace. I had a light Saturday schedule—a drive to Jefferson City to meet with college students, a conference call, some correspondence. I drove everywhere I went with windows wide open. Fresh air, seventy degrees, lots of sunlight. I was in heaven. When I got home, I changed clothes and headed for the running trails. Everyone on every bicycle I saw wore smiling faces, parents were pushing strollers, and dogs were pulling their owners with excited eagerness. What a gift.

After I came home, I spent some time on the back patio cleaning and replenishing our bird feeders. Birds of all types—Woodpeckers, Chickadees, Cardinals, Juncos, Doves, Starlings, Sparrows, and even a shy little Carolina Wren—darted and danced everywhere around me.

I was so inspired by the bright sunlight that I dared to suggest to the family that we cook outside on the grill. Uncovering the old grill, loading it with coals, and lighting it up felt like some kind of rebellion, a statement of hope and anticipation, a taunt against the winter ice and cold. I had to do something to align my spirit with the sunlight and warmth even though I know there will be much winter yet to face. Others joined my silent insurrection and one of my sons suggested we eat outdoors. Yes! Grilled burgers on the outdoor patio in the quiet of a warm, beautiful evening in the midst of winter. How cool!

In the months after his wife's death, Albert Camus wrote, "In the midst of winter, I found there was, within me, an invincible summer."* His winter was one of the soul. The light he sought was of new life, of reestablished hope, of resurrection.

Whatever the winter of your life—physical or spiritual, relational or emotional—rebel against it. With great audacity and hope and against all the odds, practice resurrection. In the midst of winter, look to the summer, the invincible summer.

Questions

- How do you rebel against darkness, despair, and hardship?
- When was a time you discovered, within you, an invincible summer?

Prayer

Keep me focused on the light, dear God, even in the darkest of moments. Keep me connected to life, to others, to you.

---

* "Return to Tipasa," in *The Myth of Sisyphus: And Other Essays*, Justin O'Brien, trans. (Vintage, 1955); p. 202. Alternate translation from French.

EMBRACING CHANGE

TRY!

16

"And the special gift of ministry you received when
I laid hands on you and prayed—keep that ablaze!
God doesn't want us to be shy with his gifts,
but bold and loving and sensible."
(2 Timothy 1:6-7, *THE MESSAGE*)

I was listening to a National Public Radio story the other day about a nihilist poet, and the reporter read some of his poems. They were marked with existential angst of the most hopeless type. The more I heard, the worse I felt. As I was driving down the road, the poems were enough to make me ask, "Why keep going down this road? Or any road?" All values are baseless, and all activity without meaning. The story went on to mention that the headstone on the poet's grave read simply, "Don't Try." It's hard to get any more cynical than that!

My thoughts went back to some comments made by several of the "under-thirty-five" leaders at a gathering one time. I asked them what they needed from older and more experienced colleagues. They described many positive role models. They spoke of older faith mentors offering them the ministry of encouragement in ways that were helpful and sustaining. Some of their older colleagues were like spiritual heroes to them, models and teachers. They had much to learn from their older peers, and they also felt they have much to teach them in return.

These young adults also described how discouraging it was for them when older persons become bitter and cynical. Comments like, "We've never done it that way before," or "We've tried that before—it'll never work." Sometimes those who are "road worn" (I count myself as one of the older ones in this story, too) come across as negative, resistant to change, stuck in old ways of doing things. It's as if some of these older people see the enthusiasm and eagerness of the younger colleagues and say, "Don't Try."

Cynicism is a kind of corrosive, slow-working poison for Christians at all levels. Cynicism declares that there are no higher motives, altruistic impulses, or worthwhile endeavors, but that all the efforts of those who seek to serve are ultimately self-serving.

I recall a writer who said, "Most people, given the choice between having a better world and having a better place within the world as it is, would choose the latter." It's hard to stay motivated to serve Christ and the community if we think everyone else around us is just serving him- or herself.

Just as isolation is a contradiction to the sacrament of Holy Communion, cynicism is a contradiction to the sacrament of baptism. With the dipping of the water, pastors who are authorized by the church to administer the sacrament and those who readily receive it are daring to remember and reclaim new birth, new life, future, possibility, the presence and sustenance of God's Spirit, resurrection. Baptism is about God saying "Yes" to us, and our allowing God's grace and affirmation to shape us. It's about hope, meaning, and the efficacy of the life of service in Christ.

Ministry in Christ's name matters. The lives we touch, the work projects we organize, the people we welcome, the dying people with whom we pray, the youth we teach, the communities we build up, the justice we proclaim, the comfort we offer—these change lives, and it is through the prayer and plans and work of pastors and laity in congregations that God transforms the world.

The Christian life matters. Our prayers, worship, study of the Word, being part of community, service, and generosity—these are the means through which Christ forms us, and through our changed lives, God seeks to change the world.

For those of us with enough experience under our belt to be a little worn and weary, please know how important it is for our younger colleagues to hear from us a word of encouragement. We all have our down times and periods of disappointment. But at the end of our years, I hope our message to the next generation is not, "Don't try."

I hope our message is, "It was worth it! Try, and try your best for the purposes of Christ. Following Christ is worth pouring your life into and giving your whole heart for, and if I could, I'd do it all again!"

Questions

- How do you overcome cynicism in your own life? In your church?
- What convinces you that life in Christ matters? That it's worth it to try to follow Christ?

Prayer

Refresh me with your Spirit, God. May others see hope in me, and new life through me.

EMBRACING CHANGE

KNOWING THAT WE KNOW

17

*"What I don't understand about myself is that I
decide one way, but then I act another, doing things
I absolutely despise. . . . I can will it, but can't do it.
I decide to do good, but I don't really do it."*
(Romans 7:15, 18-19, *THE MESSAGE*)

I heard about a church consultant who helps congregations develop strategic new initiatives and big, bold plans for their future. At the opening of the first planning session, before anyone has a clue about what proposal will finally arise from the process, he asks a couple of questions.

First, he has the leaders imagine that it is five years into the future, and the proposal they have adopted—whatever it is—has failed miserably. It didn't work and every element has disappointed. He asks them to perform the postmortem on the failed project, and to answer the question, "Why did it fail?"

Immediately people start calling out responses: It failed because it was all talk and no action, because of unclear and diffuse goals, because the laity didn't understand it or support it, because the pastor didn't push it, because the largest donors didn't contribute, because communication was bad, because it didn't reflect our mission, because we changed priorities before it could really get started, because people became distracted by other things. The list goes on and on.

Then the consultant has the leaders imagine that it is five years into the future, and the new initiative has succeeded beyond anyone's expectations. The new work has become a model for other congregations; it is changing lives, reaching new people, and extending Christ's ministry in incredible ways. Then he asks the leaders, "Why did it succeed?"

Again, the answers start coming: It succeeded because the pastor was passionate about it, because the laity loved it, because it was tied to our purpose, because it changes lives; because people kept working and never gave up, because it energized contributions, because we focused on one project as our priority. On and on the answers go. Not surprisingly, many of the answers are the reverse of the previous exercise.

What I find interesting is that without even knowing the details of the bold new plan, we already intuitively know what will make it work and what will cause it to fail. Knowing this should help us reduce the factors that lead to failure and enhance the elements that lead to success. We know the answers. We've been down these paths before.

If we know that a plan cannot succeed without passionate lay leadership, then it becomes absolutely critical to involve laity from the ground up. If we know that the plan must grow from a deep sense of mission and meet real human needs, then why not make that purpose crystal clear from the beginning? If we know that good communication is essential for success, then why not intentionally plan conversations, house meetings, and town hall gatherings for congregational feedback and engagement from the earliest stages?

On a personal level, these same dynamics are true. Imagine someone considering a personal new initiative to deepen faith and grow closer to Christ. Before we even know the details of this bold step, we may intuitively already know why it will work, or why it will fail.

"This year I'm going to read the Bible with greater frequency and intentionality . . . I'm going to help with the soup kitchen . . . I'm going to learn to pray with the help of a trusted mentor . . . I plan to sing with the praise team . . . I'm going to offer to serve as a youth sponsor . . ." The possibilities of bold action are infinite, and any one of these will deepen our knowledge of God's grace and move us forward in our walk with Christ.

If one of these is our intention, imagine that two years from now we look back and consider why the plan failed, or why it succeeded. Don't we already know?

It failed because I didn't make time for it in my schedule, because I didn't pray about it deeply enough to discern whether this was really the right thing, because it never became a priority for me, because I gave up too soon, because I tried to do it alone, because I didn't have support from my family. It failed because I relied solely upon myself. It failed because I didn't really let God in.

It succeeded because I did it together with someone else, because I made it a priority, because I stayed at it long enough to feel comfortable and competent. It succeeded because Christ in the voice of a brother or sister sustained me. It succeeded because I found the strength to change other things in my life to make it happen.

Why did it fail? Why did it succeed? Sometimes we know the answers more clearly than we realize, and knowing that we know may help us step forward more confidently than ever before.

Questions

- When have you tried something that you already knew was un- likely to succeed? Did you already know the reasons?
- What callings to service or engagement do you secretly desire to pursue? What's stopping you? What helps you move forward?

Prayer

Remove from me the internal obstacles that trip me up every time I try to serve you, Lord.

Changing Metaphors

18

"They shall beat their swords into plowshares,
and their spears into pruning hooks;
nation shall not lift up sword against nation,
neither shall they learn war any more."
(Isaiah 2:4)

Many years ago, I read a book called *Metaphors We Live By* by George Lakoff and Mark Johnson. The book transformed how I view many important elements of life.

The authors suggest that there are overarching metaphors that shape how we perceive and organize everyday realities, conceptual systems that define how we see the world. Once we accept the big-umbrella conceptual metaphor, then all our smaller word choices support the metaphor, and we get channeled into one way of seeing things that limits us to other possibilities for learning, hearing, thinking, and acting.

For instance, in our culture the predominant conceptual metaphor for disagreement is that "Argument is War." To describe our experiences we reach for the easy expressions: I *won*, you *lost*; I *attacked* her weak points; she *demolished* his argument; take your best *shot*; you could *destroy* him with this tactic; that *reinforces* my point, he can't *defend* against that, etc. Or we borrow from fighting, boxing, and shootouts: He's ready to put on the *gloves*; I'm *targeting* his weak spots; that was a *direct hit*; that idea was the *knock-out* punch; I was *saved by the bell*; you *drew blood* with that attack; and so on.

These expressions and metaphors don't just help us talk about conflict, they actually create *winners* and *losers*. They cause us to look at those with whom we disagree as *opponents*, and maybe even *enemies*, instead of partners, and make us think in terms of *losing ground* and *gaining ground*, of *victory* or *defeat*. They shape how we interpret experience and how we feel before, during, and afterwards.

Imagine if the overarching conceptual metaphor for disagreement was not war, but dance. The "Argument is Dance" conceptual framework views participants as performers. Persons play various essential and important roles, without which the dance would not be complete. One person might lead, and then another. Perhaps they have as the goal to perform in a balanced and aesthetically pleasing way. Argument would become discourse and personal expression, with each performer taking his or her steps, some planned and rehearsed and expected and others spontaneous and improvised. People finish dances exhilarated and exhausted, and wanting to do it again. There are no winners and losers, no one is defeated or destroyed, and no ground is won or lost at a dance.

Or imagine if the overarching conceptual metaphor was "Disagreement is Journey," and so we'd each step this way and that, pulling each other along and pushing each other forward toward truth. We'd focus on where we need to go, and whether we are farther along than the last time we talked. Rather than winning or losing, we might say such things as, "He really pushed you forward with that idea. Her suggestion took us a step higher. We made real progress. I feel we're getting closer and closer."

Reading that book nearly thirty years ago changed how I see conflict and argument. I confess that I also naturally fall back too often and too quickly to war metaphors for understanding disagreement in community, but I also have come to enjoy the dance and the journey. I love the exchange of ideas and how communities work things out.

For instance, whenever we proposed a new initiative in the congregation where I served as pastor, we all knew a dance would follow. Some of the same members would arrive at the dance, and take the same steps they'd learned through the years. Some would enter the discussion with a predictable and necessary skepticism, others would always delve into the financial questions, and others would keep us focused on the mission. Some made us laugh together, and that was so much their predictable role that it was as if a choreographer had written the script. New people would join us and they'd dance in styles we'd never seen, sometimes stepping on the toes of others! We all performed our steps, and someone looking down from the balcony would have applauded the intricacy, energy, and creativity we sometimes displayed. We'd finish exhausted and exhilarated, and we'd eagerly make plans for the next dance and the next time we'd meet to decide something else.

What metaphors do we use to sort out disagreement? Do we dance with our teenagers, or fight with them? If our only metaphor is war, what does victory look like? Does victory come by destroying? Everybody survives a dance.

Do we dance with those who see the world differently, or try to knock them out?

Here's the thing about these metaphors: If we expect war, then war we find, and it becomes impossible to see our interchanges in any other way. But if we expect dance, something more graceful may result. If we expect journey, then maybe we move a few steps further along in our following of Christ.

EMBRACING CHANGE

Questions

- What does it feel like to win a significant disagreement with someone we love? How does it feel to lose? How helpful are the words *winning* and *losing* for describing our experience and goal with people we love?
- With whom do you need to rethink the metaphors of disagreement?

Prayer

Dear Lord, with those I love, help me to discover progress not in winning but in learning and loving.

THE FIELD

19

"So let's not allow ourselves to get fatigued doing good.
At the right time we will harvest a good crop
if we don't give up, or quit."
(Galatians 6:9, *THE MESSAGE*)

With binoculars in hand, I entered the field seeking a better angle to see the mix of sparrows stealthily foraging in a brush pile. The field, jointly owned and managed by the conservation department and a local farmer, had evidently lain fallow for a season. I quietly walked around the brush pile, identifying White-Crowned, White-Throated, Field, and American Tree Sparrows. After the sparrow pack moved on, I turned and faced the field.

A thought occurred to me. What if someone unexpectedly gave me this field in its current condition with the expectation that I would deliver a harvest? What would I do?

First, whatever I were to do would involve a long, slow process. You cannot give me a field like this one day and expect that the next day I will produce bushels of corn or truckloads of pumpkins. Unless I climb a fence and steal the neighbor's corn, I will have nothing to show for some time. Starting from this point, it will take months to evidence any noticeable harvest. Cultivation takes time and the passing of seasons, and requires patience without cynicism or resignation.

Second, since I know little about farming, I would have much learning to do. I'd want to know about my field—soil studies, agricultural studies, climate studies, water studies, and market studies. There's no sense planting banana trees in Missouri or rice in Arizona. I'd need to learn from other farmers. I'd talk with them, watch them, ask their advice, see what works for them, and pattern my work after theirs. Yet studying and learning does not bring a harvest.

Third, I'd get to work, doing something each day to move toward the harvest. The kind and volume of work that fills my days would differ from season to season. Some work would involve tilling the soil, enriching the soil, planting the seed at the right time. Other times involve cultivation, watering, protecting from pests and rodents and weeds. Other times require harvesting at the time of perfect ripeness and readiness, and then immediately doing the "groundwork" for the following season.

Fourth, I'd have to attend to timing. Some periods require repressively long hours of urgent work and other periods involve simply reading and learning more. There are times of ripeness and readiness I dare not miss, seasons of unusual and unrepeating opportunity. Some evenings I'd have lights on my harvest as I worked through the night, not because that's my preferred schedule, but because the ripeness of the crop or the changing weather requires it.

Fifth, I'd have to learn to live with mixed and inconsistent results. There are good seasons and bad, harvests that exceed expectations and others that disappoint. I'd take the long view, and trust that if I repeated the right actions year after year, that harvests will come, some large, some mediocre, and some small.

Scripture is replete with images of seeds and sowers, farmers and soils, seedtime and harvest, vines and branches. The biblical writers remind us of the patience and hard work required, and of the risks of birds and rocks and weeds. They also steady our fears with the promise and hope of harvests, some thirty-fold, some sixty-fold, and some a hundred-fold.

These metaphors describe our souls. We've each been given a field. Our personal work is difficult and lifelong, the risks are many, and fruitfulness is expected. How do we till and re-till the soil, plant the right seeds, protect against the weeds and pests, and offer fruit pleasing to our Lord? God's is a Spirit of assurance, of vision, of sustenance, a present help in trouble. We do not garden alone. God is the Lord of the harvest.

These metaphors also speak of our congregations. How are we doing with the hard work of preparation, of cultivating the hearts and minds and souls of people? Are we studying our soil, learning from others, and doing the right things to bring forth fruitful congregations?

And then there is the mission field. Each of our churches has been entrusted with a field, the community of people that surround us, the large numbers of people who do not know Christ. The mission field also includes countless people who suffer from loneliness, poverty, racism, or violence. This field provides the mission and purpose for our work, and we serve in obedience to Christ and out of love for neighbor and for God. How are we learning about this field and how best to bring forth its yield? How are we protecting, cultivating, and caring for the mission field? Our purpose as a church is the mission field.

We've each been given a field. The contours of our souls provide rich possibilities for cultivation, and we see in the lives of others what we can become by the grace of God. We're also members of congregations who have been entrusted with fields of possibility and potential.

God has placed us in these fields for a purpose, and gives us the promise of rich harvests.

Questions

- How does your own soul feel like a field? How do you cultivate and care for it? What are the seeds? The risks? The harvest?
- Describe the mission field your congregation has been given. What are the seeds, the risks, and the harvest?

Prayer

Ripen in me the expectation of serving you fruitfully, Lord, all the days of my life.

WHEN YOU ARE
THROUGH CHANGING . . .

20

"How can anyone," said Nicodemus, "be born
who has already been born and grown up?"
(John 3:4, *THE MESSAGE*)

As I sat in a pastor's office, I noticed a small, etched sign he kept on his desk. It read, "When you are through changing . . . you're through!"

At first I smiled. The saying reminds me of many I've seen before. I remember a poster from my high school days that said much the same thing: "He who isn't busy being born is busy dying." I recalled when one of my sons was a preschooler and adopted some new behavior, how I had described to an older member of my church, "He's going through a transition right now." The member, who had children older than I, chuckled and said, "Robert, your kids will always be going through a transition for as long as you live!" She was right!

As I thought a little deeper about the truth of the message on the pastor's desk, I realized that change is life, future, hope, resurrection. I also realized that change is stressful, hard, painful, and involves grief and mourning. Ronald Heifetz once said that people don't fear change, they fear loss.* When we change, we leave behind old familiar things—ways of doing things, patterns, habits, attitudes, behaviors that are comfortable.

Change takes faith. Abraham and Sarah, the Letter to Hebrews reminds us, "stepped out not knowing where they were going" (11:8). Stepping out not knowing where we are going—that's what happens every time a couple gets married, every time parents have a baby, every time a child goes to school on the first day of kindergarten or a young person heads off to college. That's what happens when people lean into the future, reach out to others, open their hearts and minds and doors. Change happens. And it's not easy. But it is life. "When you're through changing . . . you're through."

Forward movement in our following of Christ comes as we co-operate with the Holy Spirit in our own maturation and growth. God's Spirit is calling us toward greater Christ-likeness. We starve the old nature and feed the new creation as we intentionally move toward Christ. Change and growth are essential elements of our spiritual growth and discipleship.

I remember an older woman, a friend from a church I served, who found great delight in studying Spanish. She attended classes, practiced with friends, had a tutor, read books, and used her ever-increasing fluency in service to the church and to others through her involvement in missions and hospitality. She was a saint.

She learned that she had cancer. She fought it bravely, won some time, but eventually the cancer recurred. Her last months were spent in hospice care. She and everyone who loved her knew the inevitable outcome. While she was in hospice care during the last weeks of her life, I stepped into her room one day to find her repetitiously writing out Spanish grammar exercises. She was preparing for her tutor to arrive, and was cramming the last bits of homework that was due.

Stop for a minute and think about this with me. She has only a few weeks to live, and she knows it. For what purpose was she learning Spanish verb tenses? She was doing it, I feel, because growing, learning, practicing, improving, changing—these were for her the ultimate signs of life. They were her expression of faith and hope, even in the face of death. Change and growth are life.

"When you're through changing . . . you're through."

Questions

- How are you a different person now from three years ago?
- How do you cooperate with the Holy Spirit in the maturing of your faith? Do you feel closer to God now than three years ago? Are you on a path that will take you closer during the years to come?

Prayer

Make me over again and again, Lord, until my life becomes fully an instrument of your gracious and perfect love.

---

* *Leadership on the Line* (Harvard Business School Press, 2002); p. 11.

5

LETTING GO

VESTIGES

21

"So if anyone is in Christ, there is a new creation;
everything old has passed away;
see, everything has become new!"
(2 Corinthians 5:17)

Years ago, while I was serving as pastor of a congregation in Texas, the church decided to repaint and refinish the entire sanctuary, including the pews. These pews had been installed in the late 1920's and early 1930's, and were lengthy, heavy, and well-built. I hosted various woodworkers, furniture refinishers, and other craftsmen as we were taking bids on the project. At one of these meetings, I crawled under the pews and noticed that each pew, beneath each seat-width, had a wire rack attached. There were hundreds of these in the sanctuary, unseen by anyone for years. The racks were screwed closely to the wood's surface, under each and every seat. Imagine sitting in a pew, leaning forward, reaching between your knees up under your seat—that's what you'd need to do to touch one of these racks. Any idea what they were for?

It took me a few minutes when I first saw them. And then I started to laugh. These were men's hat racks! They were designed for people with Western hats (welcome to Texas!) with wide brims to slip their hats upside down underneath their seats. While they were used regularly in the 1930's, these racks probably had not been used a single time in the last fifty years.

The hat racks were vestiges of a bygone era. A vestige is a visible trace, evidence, or sign of something that once existed or served a purpose, but does so no more. The discovery of the hat racks caused me to look around at other vestiges, and I found that our church was full of them. There were furnishings, cabinets, and accessories in our foyer that no one ever used.

Some of these vestiges are quaint and humorous. On the other hand, they should give us pause to think about why we do what we do. Someone shared a story about how their church worked with the Five Practices. Church leaders walked through the building to talk about how a visitor might view the facility. Before they began, they brainstormed about the foyer, asking themselves, "What are the most important things to have in the entryway to help visitors?" They suggested an information booth, a display of brochures about ministries, a bulletin board full of photos that invites people to upcoming events. They even considered a rocking chair for parents of infants who need to step out from the sanctuary. The leaders then walked through the foyer to see what they currently had in this important space for new impressions.

In the foyer was a large glass case with a huge Memorial Book that records gifts to the Memorial Fund. The last entry was nearly twenty years old! They found a heavy pedestal with a Visitor Registration Book stuck in a dark corner. The book was unused. They found a case holding usher identification buttons that hadn't been used in years. In short, they found vestiges of another era.

Courageously, the congregational leaders changed the entryway to serve the purposes and needs of the church today. They moved some things to other places in the church, did away with other things altogether, and added what they needed to make the space useful, positive, and appealing for welcoming newcomers and longtime members. They added more light, painted the walls a lighter color, and made the space open and inviting.

We find vestiges in every aspect of life. (What are those buttons for on the cuff of a man's suit?) Even spiritual practices that formerly had great meaning become mere vestiges when they lose their power and significance.

Our family holds hands before each meal and recites together a brief rhyming prayer. We've done that since our sons were children, and we continue even though they are now both taller than I. On the one hand, I value the prayer for its simplicity, the unifying quality of this tradition for our family. On the other hand, we sometimes move through it quickly by rote, hardly pausing even for a second to think about its meaning. Is the prayer still a valid way to acknowledge God, to genuinely give thanks for the gift of life and to express our dependence upon God for all things? Or is it a vestige, a visible trace or sign of something that once served a purpose, but does so no more?

Think about some of your own personal faith practices. How many have become so routine that they are at risk of losing their value and purpose? Occasionally, it's helpful to rethink why we do what we do, and to consider how to renew these practices so that they connect us to God and to others in ways that fit our current life.

Question

- How do you keep your daily practices of morning prayers, dinner prayers, or nightly prayers alive and fresh?

Prayer

With you, Lord, we get a fresh start, we're created new. Help us abandon ways that no longer work, and take up practices that bind us to you and to others with purpose and vitality.

THANK YOU, KATHLEEN

22

*"For I am convinced that neither death, nor life,
nor angels, nor rulers, nor things present, nor things to
come, nor powers, nor height, nor depth, nor anything else
in all creation, will be able to separate us from the love of
God in Christ Jesus our Lord."*
(Romans 8:38-39)

As I was leaving the office recently, an email message delivered the news that Kathleen Baskin-Ball had died. Kathleen was a United Methodist pastor, a mother, a wife, a friend. She had undergone cancer treatments for months, suffering and celebrating through the ups and downs, the hopeful rises and disappointing setbacks. The report I received from friends earlier was that options were increasingly limited for Kathleen, and that time was short. And yet nobody thought this day would come so quickly.

Kathleen and I shared a mutual respect and regard from afar, a tacit but deep understanding that we were kindred spirits, that we valued many of the same things and shared a common vision about the most fundamental issues of life and ministry. Even though our conversations were few and brief over many years, she always impressed me as someone I wanted to know better, to work alongside more closely, to learn from and grow with. She had this effect on many people. She evoked from people a confidence in her leadership, a trust about her competence and motivation that was unquestionable and genuine. Her ministry was real, rooted in a rich interior life and a deeply personal faith in Christ and pouring herself out in ways that changed lives and mobilized people. Through lives shaped by her spirit and nurtured by her leadership, communities were transformed. Like Paul, she willingly became "all things to all people" in order to reach them with the gift and demand of God's grace: learning Spanish to serve across cultures; working in the inner city to break through walls of race and class; serving with equally wonderful fruitfulness both an edgy, progressive congregation and a suburban growth congregation. Two days before her death, she baptized a room full of babies, blessed friends, and offered encouragement to those who came to encourage her.

Hearing of her passing brought forth in me a rush of feelings and stimulated a host of memories of other colleagues, and their deaths too young: Eric, Mary, Susan, Jim, and Robert. Part of the tragedy in each case was the sense of unfulfilled promise, a gnawing, smoldering feeling of unfairness, that they, and we, and all who loved them, and all whose lives they would certainly have touched had been unjustly robbed, wrongfully plundered of an unfathomable treasure.

I last saw Kathleen at Jurisdictional Conference. Her ongoing health struggles and the experimental quality of her treatment were no secret. We were in the large banquet hall as the delegates moved toward a break. We pulled aside from the crowd for a few minutes of personal conversation. I felt the need to say something about her illness, about her being in my prayers, about my grieving her not being among the candidates for Bishop, about my hope that one day she'd be past all this and that we'd have more enjoyable conversations. It felt awkward, and my words didn't flow as I would have wanted, and emotion tightened my throat. I knew. She knew. This would likely be our last conversation. While I was stammering to say what I needed to say, she looked me in the eye, smiled, and said, "You know, Robert, it's going to be all right. I'm at peace." My sputtering attempts to minister to her ended in her ministering to me. The awkwardness disappeared. I relaxed. We chatted for a few minutes more. We talked about family and ministry and mutual friends. We parted with a hug, and expressed our mutual desire to one day have the chance to spend more time together and work alongside each other. In her response to my question about her health, it's as if she provided a profound summary of our faith: "I'm dying. But I'm fine."

Eric, Mary, Susan, Jim, Robert, and Kathleen lived lives that were bigger than their untimely deaths. They knew "the life that really is life"; they tasted of its abundance and shared in its delights. They knew what it is to love and to be loved, and to find a sense of satisfaction and meaning in their contribution to others. They laughed with those who laughed and cried with those who cried. Through all their steps forward, sidesteps, missteps, detours, and false starts, they endeavored to follow Christ, and our lives have been made richer by their sharing their journeys with us.

Frederick Buechner tells of an aged monk who outlived all his friends and family, who was asked about the grief he had tasted so many times in their passing. His response: "What's lost is nothing to what's found, and all the death there ever was, set next to life, would scarcely fill a cup."*

Thank you, Kathleen, for your life, your ministry, and your friendship. Thank you, Lord, for the gift of life unending and eternal, and for the witness and ministry of Kathleen Baskin-Ball.

Question
- When has someone you sought to console actually consoled you? What are the elements of grace and character that make it possible to accept death as part of God's plan for life?

Prayer
Thank you, Lord, for all those we hold in our hearts who are gone from our touch.

---

* *Godric* (HarperOne, 1983); p. 96.

STAY BACK

23

"You're here to be light, bringing out
the God-colors in the world."
(Matthew 5:14, *THE MESSAGE*)

Recently, I heard the sirens of an emergency vehicle approaching from behind me, and so I slowed down and moved to the side of the road. A large fire engine passed me with lights flashing. As it drove by me, I noticed a number of decals highly visible around the various compartments, doors, knobs, switches around the truck. And as it moved ahead of me, I saw the huge reflective sign on the rear of the vehicle that read: "Stay Back 200 Feet."

I can easily imagine why this sign is necessary. As firefighters do their work at an accident scene, a rescue operation, or a house fire, they need plenty of room to maneuver and they don't want interference by non-professionals, onlookers, and wannabe helpers. "Stay Back 200 Feet" makes good sense on the rear of a fire truck.

This stimulated some thoughts about other places I've seen similar signs, but not in bright reflective paint and decals. I remember a friend in school who might as well have worn a sign around his neck "Stay Back 200 Feet" everywhere he went. He had an explosive temper, and he used his anger to manipulate people. Being around him required walking on eggshells, trying to be careful not to set him off.

Everyone was fearful of saying or doing the wrong thing, and so they tried to please him to avoid conflict. Or they simply stood back a couple hundred feet and avoided him! As the years unfolded, ministry didn't work out well for him.

Some people are so task-focused that they unintentionally push people away, and others carry such a negative and dark cynicism that people purposefully avoid them. Sometimes parents so intensely pursue their careers and their personal hobbies, that without realizing it, they signal to their children, "Stay back. Leave me alone. My work is more important than you. Find your own way."

What signs do you wear and what signals do you send to those you love, those with whom you work, and those whom you encounter daily?

Churches also can have signs that read "Stay Back 200 Feet" but most of them don't realize it. For parents with young children, a church that has an overgrown, unkempt, dangerous-looking playground has a sign that reads, "Run Away and Take Your Children With You!" A church with a confusing choice of solid wooden doors facing the parking lot and with no signage indicating where to enter in effect sends a signal to visitors that says, "Stay Back! Enter at Your Own Risk! You're on Your Own." A church located away from the main roads and without directional signs on nearby streets might as well say, "Stay Away! We're Hiding! Good Luck. Bring a Compass!" A congregation without a plan for welcoming visitors and following up with further contact might as well pass out lapel buttons to its members that read, "Keep Your Distance! Don't Interfere in Our Family Gathering! Stay Away!"

Jesus was a sign from God, a signal of God's desire to reach us, to love us, and to bring us back. Jesus' message revealing God's nature was not "Stay Back," but "Come Follow." Jesus' life, death, and resurrection was a sign of God's love for the world and everyone in it. Jesus, Scripture suggests, was an ensign to God's people, a flag that signaled God's love and welcome and embrace.

Jesus invites us to be signs. In fact, he asks to be shining neon lights that reflect the life we see in him. Jesus says, "You're here to be light, bringing out the God-colors in the world. God is not a secret to be kept. We're going public with this . . . Shine! Keep open house; be generous with your lives. By opening up to others, you'll prompt people to open up with God, this generous Father in heaven" (Matthew 5:14, 16, *THE MESSAGE*).

What's our sign? "Welcome in the Name of Christ"? Or, "Stay Back 200 Feet"?

Questions
- What sign do we wear and what signals do you send to family members? To coworkers? To strangers?
- What sign and signal does your community see from your congregation?

Prayer
Help me reflect your gracious love, dear God, rather than my own fears and self-preoccupations.

Paradox

24

*"Immediately the father of the child cried out,
'I believe; help my unbelief.'"*
(Mark 9:24)

I love writing. Nothing exhilarates the mind like the unexpected striking of a new idea. New ideas bring a powerful emotional and intellectual adrenaline rush, and I love to feel the eagerness to get a thought down on paper before it slips away, the quick abbreviated words on note cards, the illegible outlines on napkins. And I love the generative process, the creative exercise of taking loose ideas, unfinished ideas, and little broken pieces of ideas and moving them around on paper, trying to get a tapestry to take shape, waiting and working to see what will appear. Finally, and perhaps most of all, I love the sense of contribution and achievement that comes with the finished work, the positive responses from readers, the nodding heads that indicate understanding, and the "aha" moments that people experience and report back to me. Then I know that my writing matters; it is worth it. I love writing.

Also, I hate writing. Nothing so oppresses me as having a deadline for an article or a blog or a chapter, and having absolutely nothing to say. I abhor the convicting quality of a blank computer screen reminding me of my own emptiness, my lack of creativity, my failings at innovation or improvisation. I hate useless and silly ideas that intrude uninvited into my mind when I've got work to do, and I resent the way untamed thoughts distract me from my job and steal away my leisure. These unbidden ideas make me record their presence on messy note cards that I despise having to carry around, and they even push me into scribbling outlines on paper napkins. And nothing so disheartens me as facing the hard reality that I can't write today, that never again will I have a decent idea worth recording. And nothing pains me more than the awareness that people read what I write, and they see how lame my ideas are. Then I know that my writing is not worth the trouble, and I should quit forever. I hate writing.

Before you call a doctor for me, let me suggest that the two paragraphs above are not signs of a totally schizophrenic personality. Rather they capture the paradox of most creative undertakings. These paragraphs express the way I feel about many of the most important endeavors, tasks, duties, and joys of my life. I love preparing sermons, and I also find it incredibly difficult at times. I enjoy visiting the sick, working on mission teams, preparing for meetings, presenting new ideas, and I also detect many internal resistances to doing these things. I love working with people, and I also find it draining and hard to do. I adore my sons, and I also become totally exasperated by them. Nothing refreshes me like a nice, long evening run, and yet just the thought seems an oppressive burden.

Paradox means two distinct, opposing ideas that are absurdly contradictory, but may actually both be true, and our efforts to resolve the inconsistencies may take us down futile paths. The call of God we discern for us to work for God's purposes is packed with paradox. Every prompting of the Holy Spirit to make a positive difference in the lives of people also stimulates negative internal resistance, doubt, and fear. God asked Moses to return to Egypt to set free a people who were already a part of Moses' own heart. Moses stuttered out his excuses: "I can't speak well enough. I'm not worthy. No one will listen to me. Please send someone else." He both wanted to do it, and hated to do it. Moses was exhilarated as well as overwhelmed; enlivened by the possibilities as well as defeated by his own sense of inadequacy. Did he want to go, or did he not want to go? Both were true. Paradox. "Lord, I believe; help my unbelief."

I know physicians who love the challenge of figuring out what leads to healing and relief from suffering. They feel drawn to help others; they love people. They also feel repelled by the deep anguish of suffering, of seeing unbelievable horror at times. One doctor who works on a children's cancer ward told me she can hardly make herself go to work in the morning, but then she loves what she does so much that she can hardly come home from work at night. She loves it. She hates it. It's a calling of God. Many teachers, social workers, youth sponsors, mission volunteers, and church workers could say the same.

Ministry is hard work, a sweet passion as well as an exhausting duty. Leading youth, singing with a praise band, serving on the Trustees, visiting the elderly, working in missions—these give us life and also drive us crazy.

That's OK. Following Christ involves giving in order to receive, loving those we hate, listening for wisdom from children, praying for those who persecute us, losing in order to gain, and a whole host of other paradoxes, including dying in order to live.

Give God thanks for the paradoxes, and for the strength and motivation to show up and get to work nevertheless.

Questions

- What significant work do you paradoxically both enjoy and resist?
- How do you overcome the doubts, resistances, and excuses to do what is fruitful and satisfying?

Prayer

To my desire to serve you and others, Lord, may the resistances and doubts within me lend humility rather than paralysis.

REDEEMING TIME

25

"Martha, Martha, you are worried and
distracted by many things; there is need of
only one thing. Mary has chosen the better part."
(Luke 10:41-42)

Remember that film *The Terminal* starring Tom Hanks where he gets snagged with immigration issues and ends up living in an airport terminal for months? Well, that's what I felt like recently. I intended a quick in-and-out trip to Newark to visit with clergy and laity about the book *Five Practices of Fruitful Congregations*. Instead, I ended up stuck in Newark watching one flight after another to St. Louis get delayed, then delayed again, and finally cancelled. This meant I had to stay an extra night in Newark, and then another night. Fourteen flights in a row that had my name on them were cancelled. During that time, I was snowed in and lived in an airport hotel with the courtesy shuttle providing my only entertainment, taking me back and forth between hotel and terminal. Each day I'd spend about six hours at the airport standing in line and talking to airline representatives in person and travel agents by phone. I ate four consecutive hotel club sandwiches. I did make one free trip on the hotel shuttle to the airport just to grab something from the airport food court for a little variation. It's pretty bad when you look forward to the gourmet at the airport food court to add a little pizzazz to your diet!

As soon as I realized I was stuck, I began to cancel things. I rescheduled five appointments I had planned for Friday, and sent word that I may not make it to Kansas City on Saturday morning and Springfield on Saturday afternoon for Confirmation Days worship services. I was supposed to visit with the leaders of a congregation on Saturday evening, preach four times on Sunday in Springfield, and visit with another congregation Sunday afternoon. I sent out the "heads up" that I might not make it.

I tried everything to change flight plans, pursue options, and to figure out how to get home. I overheard some of my fellow travelers making elaborate plans, such as taking a 19-hour train ride to Chicago and then driving from Chicago to St. Louis. Another was planning to fly Newark to Washington, then Atlanta, then to Nashville, and then rent a car to drive to St. Louis. I could sympathize with their frustration and their desire to try anything. Sometimes it seems like doing something is better than just waiting and doing nothing. But nothing is all any of us could really do. Years ago when I found myself churning and churning to make things happen in a situation over which I had no control, I remember someone telling me, "Robert, don't just do something; sit there!"

And so back at the hotel I sat. I walked a bunch of treadmill miles in the little fitness center. I read a newspaper for the first time in a month. I caught up on my journal. I fell asleep the first night at 10 P.M. and didn't wake up until 9 A.M. That's eleven hours. Maybe my body was trying to tell me something. I read a paperback novel, and drank hot tea, and paced, and made phone calls until my battery ran low. Mostly, I waited.

Here's the irony: I was so frustrated and exasperated at being stuck against my will for two days. On the other hand, for the last two months I've desperately wanted a couple of uninterrupted days for writing. But I couldn't write. My attitude was keeping me from enjoying and making good use of this enforced period of rest. I didn't like it, and I struggled against it, but there was nothing I could do. My spiritual agitation was keeping me from receiving an unexpected gift.

John Wesley wrote a tract entitled, "On Redeeming the Time." When you actually stop to think about it, redeeming our time is redeeming our life. By redeeming our time, I don't mean filling every single second to overflowing with tasks and achievements, with work and busyness. I mean making time sacred, useful to God, holy. Or maybe it's better to say, redeeming the time involves discovering the holy, the gift-like quality, the grace of time. It involves perceiving time differently, looking at time through God's eyes.

Sometimes we rush along on the horizontal plane, pushing, pressing, all forward motion, doing and doing and doing. The tyranny of the urgent stifles creativity, reflection, rumination. Mary and Martha taught us that, didn't they? Which one of the two women made the wisest choice? Both of them are inside of us daily. And Jesus told his disciples, "Come away to a place by yourselves and rest awhile." I suspect that was not an invitation to laziness, but to reflection, renewal, rejuvenation, resurrection. Sometimes God has a way of reminding us, "Don't just do something, sit there." Breathe in a little sabbath. It's a gift God gives us, and sometimes we don't get it until events bring our busyness to a screeching halt.

Questions

- When have unexpected circumstances and interruptions turned your attention toward the sacred? Have you ever faced a "forced" sabbath? How did you handle it?
- When is time a gift for you? When is it a burden? How do you make time useful to God, and what does that mean for you?

Prayer

Dear God, help me know the meaning of the time I've been given, and to use it wisely both to adore you and to serve you in healthy proportions.

6

REACHING OUT

PRAY FOR PEACE

26

". . . to guide our feet into the way of peace."
(Luke 1:79)

As I was driving down a city street, I noticed a car that had a bumper sticker that read simply, "Pray for Peace." When we approached a stoplight, I pulled up beside the car and saw that the driver wore the sandy brown camouflage uniform of the U.S. Army.

I suppose that if I placed a bumper sticker on my car that said, "Pray for Peace," people might project onto me any number of political motivations. They might suspect me of being unsupportive of those families who have loved ones in the service. They might presume a particular political leaning, a partisan perspective. But when this young officer in the car beside me, who has offered himself in service to his country, reminds us to pray for peace, he does so with an integrity and authenticity that is hard to match.

Join me in praying for peace. Our faith finds its roots in the hope for a day when "the lion shall sleep with the lamb." We serve a Lord who said, "Peace I leave with you, my peace I give to you." For nearly two thousand years, we have offered "grace and peace" to one another when we gather in Christ's name after the example of our early Christian forebears of faith. Peace is our hope, our prayer, our yearning, our aim, our end.

Whether you vote Republican, Democrat, Independent, or don't vote at all—pray for peace. Whether you are fiercely patriotic or suspicious of nationalistic impulses, whether you are new to the faith or long established, whether you support strategies that call for a troop surge, immediate removal, or gradual disengagement—pray for peace. Whether you are career military, have loved ones in the service, or have no personal connections at all to the military—pray for peace. Whether you are conservative, liberal, middle of the road, old, young, middle-aged—pray for peace. The yearning for peace knows no national, ethnic, gender, or age boundaries. The gift and demand of peace requires something from everyone.

Sometimes church leaders, pastors, and vocal Christian lay leaders are criticized for supporting or promoting particular strategies, policies, or agendas. Sometimes these criticisms are justified because there are diverse paths and conflicting opinions about how best to achieve some of the outcomes that reflect the core of our faith. But while we may disagree about strategies, policies, and agendas, there are certain basic visions that God calls all of us to pursue. There may be various pathways that take us there, but all of us should yearn in our souls for peace, for justice, for the elimination of suffering, of hunger, of poverty, of sickness, and of racism.

We love children because Jesus loved children, and Jesus reveals the heart of God. We love justice because Jesus loved justice, and Jesus reveals the will of God. We love peace because Jesus loved peace, and Jesus reveals the mind of God.

Will there ever be peace throughout the world? As long as there is original sin, there will be violence and responses to violence, bloodshed and attempts to limit, avoid, protect, and heal from bloodshed. Will we ever agree to a single policy, strategy, or plan for peace? Probably not, given our varying experiences, perspectives, and commitments. But as to the direction, goal, vision, and commitment of our lives, we should lean toward a future marked by peace. That's part of what it means to be the people of the Way.

Join with the anonymous soldier in the car with the bumper sticker. For God's sake, "Pray for Peace."

Questions

- How do you pray for peace? How does praying for peace shape you?
- How does praying for peace change anything in the world?

Prayer

In my family, my workplace, my community, my church, and your world, make me an instrument of your peace, Lord. Let it begin with me.

THE EYES SAY IT ALL

27

"My relatives and close friends have failed me;
the guests in my house have forgotten me,
my serving girls count me as a stranger;
I have become an alien in their eyes."
(Job 19:14-15)

I heard my friend and colleague Sally Dyck preach an excellent sermon on one of the Five Practices, Radical Hospitality, which she began with the line, "It's in the eyes. The eyes say it all." She went on to tell about the way we look at people, and the messages we send by how we look at them. Bishop Dyck's sermon has lingered with me, and I've found myself thinking about it many times since.

Luke 15 opens with the tax collectors and sinners drawing near to listen to Jesus. The Scribes and Pharisees grumbled, saying, "This man receives sinners and eats with them." Can you picture the people who would say this? They didn't have to grumble out loud to make their opinions known. Imagine how they glared at the outsiders, despising them, judging and condemning with every glance. Hard eyes. Rejecting eyes.

What was in the eyes of the people reaching for rocks to stone the woman caught in adultery? Can you see the cold, predatory intensity? Can you see in their eyes the hatred, the intense anger toward her that refocused on Jesus when he interceded on her behalf? What did she see in Jesus' eyes compared to what she saw in all the others? Compassion? Understanding? Steel resolve?

What was in the eyes of the proud who walked the streets with their expensive robes swaying behind them to impress all the commoners? What kind of condescension and distaste were in the eyes of the rich man when he looked through his mansion gates to the pitiful Lazarus, sick and begging on the streets outside? The eyes say it all.

On the other hand, what did Jesus' eyes say to Zacchaeus that brought him down from the tree he had shinnied up to avoid the rejection of the community? What love was there in those eyes that pierced Zacchaeus' heart so profoundly that he completely reversed the course of his life, finally accepting that he was accepted and loved by God?

What did the woman at the well think when Jesus' eyes didn't overlook her like she wasn't even there? What did she see in his eyes that made her feel safe and comfortable speaking to him?

With our eyes we judge, convict, reject, and accuse. People can see when we feel suspicious, or superior, or fearful. Worst of all, by the casting of our eyes we can totally ignore, fail to notice, and treat someone like they don't even exist.

When I stopped to pick up clothes at the drycleaners, my cell phone rang as I stepped from my car. Taking the call, I paced back and forth for several minutes in the parking lot talking on the phone. After I finished, I walked into the cleaners. The young man behind the counter immediately thanked me. I didn't understand why he was thanking me, and he saw the puzzled look on my face. He said, "Thanks for finishing the call before coming inside. Sometimes people come in talking on their phones or texting, and they never say a word to us or even look up. They give us their ticket, pay their bill, take their clothes and leave. I feel invisible. It's a bit humiliating."

Our eyes build someone up, or tear someone down. They confer blessing or curse. Eyes smile. They welcome. They affirm. They accept. They care. They give life. Or they growl. Condemn. Punish. Exclude. Looks can kill.

What do our eyes say when our Goth niece shows up at the family reunion, complete with stark black hair and studded leather bracelet? Do our eyes say, "Please leave," or "We're glad you're here"? Do they say, "We love you only when you do things our way," or "We love you always"?

What do our eyes communicate to a mom when her baby fusses in church, or to the child who drops a coin that rolls beneath the pews all the way to the front? What messages do our children receive through our eyes when they take the tattoo detour and the piercing path through their young adult years? The cousin reconstructing his life for the third time after rehab—does he see in our eyes total disdain and eternal rejection, or does he see a glimpse of genuine encouragement, a prayerful hopefulness? The young men and women carrying camouflage backpacks and wearing service fatigues whom we see in our airports heading for the front lines or returning for leave, what do they see in our eyes looking at them? Support? Concern? Judgment? Pity? Respect?

Many of our prayers ask God to *change our hearts*. Sometimes we courageously follow God's calling into circumstances that *change our minds*. We have prayers to *change our spirits*: "Lord, put a new and right spirit within me."

Maybe we also need a prayer that says, "Lord, change the way I look at people. Remove from me the unwarranted looks of impatience, dissatisfaction, and disapproval, and replace them with your countenance."

Questions

- When has the way someone has looked at you pushed you away? When has someone's eyes welcomed you and built you up?
- How does your congregation, or your family, look upon those who are different?

Prayer

Help me see the world through your eyes, Lord, and remake me so that people see you in my eyes.

A Simple Invitation

28

*"Nathanael said to him, 'Can anything good come out of
Nazareth?' Philip said to him, 'Come and see.' "*
(John 1:46)

I stopped by a small business and was assisted by a young man
who had to take some information from me—name, address, em-
ployment, etc. When I said I worked for the church, he smiled and
said, "Really? I grew up in the Methodist church," and he told me
about his home church. I knew his pastor, and we spoke fondly of his
ministry. Later as we were finishing our transaction, I asked him if he
was attending a church here in town. He said that he and his fiancée
had not yet found a church. In reality, they hadn't visited one yet,
even though they had lived here for three years. This led me to ask a
few more questions, and when I heard more about his fiancée's religious background, I suggested two possible churches that seemed to
me to offer the kind of ministry and services that might match their
situation. I talked a little about each one. He seemed interested and
asked a few questions about both of the churches. As we parted ways,
I gently encouraged him to give one or the other of the churches a
visit, and he seemed appreciative of the encouragement.

As I walked away, a few thoughts occurred to me. First, this conversation was easy, positive, and mutually encouraging (despite the

fact that I'm an extreme introvert and do not enter easily into conversations with strangers!). I wondered why I do this so infrequently. What internal resistances keep me from speaking like this in other situations? Maybe I should do it more intentionally and consistently. If I can do this, so can just about anyone. So can you. Second, if I intentionally repeat this sort of interaction once a week, perhaps in a year at least a couple of people might actually visit a church because of it, people who might otherwise not do so. Like the sower scattering seed, most of these conversations would come to nothing. But by the grace of God, some seed might find fertile soil and take root. Third, if even a small fraction of the people in our congregations offered such an invitation more regularly, the results could be remarkable. God uses ordinary practices to accomplish extraordinary miracles in the life of people.

Finally, I pledged to do this more frequently and consistently. Rather than committing myself to the huge and nebulous goal of somehow "bearing witness to Christ in the world," I decided to try to cultivate at least one conversation each week to gently nudge someone toward a relationship with a church. I found myself wondering about and praying for what the experience might be if this young couple should actually show up for services at one of our churches. Would they feel welcome? Would they feel connected to others and to God? Would someone from the church follow up with real interest in their lives, their faith journeys, their relationship to God?

Recently, I had a long conversation with a pastor serving her first appointment. She was searching for ideas about how to invite people into the life of the church. I asked her a few questions about her own weekly schedule, and eventually asked her, "Where in the course of a week do you have significant contact with people who are not members of your church, or who are not other pastors or members of other churches? Where does your life intersect significantly with people who have no church?" She had to think about this for a long time. It finally dawned on her that the demands of the local church had so insulated her that she rarely had significant contact with people outside the congregation. So we talked about her hobbies, interests, clubs, sororities, civic and service groups, sports activities. I suggested that she "get a life" (this was said more gently and positively than that sounds!) outside of the local church in order to develop the sort of relationships and friendships and acquaintances that could lead to authentic invitation. Her predicament mirrors the lives of many of our pastors and laity alike. God came to us and became like us to reach us in Christ, but sometimes it's easy to forget that we have to go to others where they are to reach them.

Countless lifelong journeys of faith have begun with a simple invitation from a friend or stranger.

Questions

- How do you offer the authentic and gentle invitation to others to a ministry of your church? How do you personally say, "Come and see"?
- If everyone in your congregation invited people with the same frequency and consistency as you do, would your church grow or decline?
- Who are the people among whom God has placed you in order to offer such an invitation?

Prayer

Give me courage, dear God, to care enough to offer your invitation.

REACHING OUT

SEEDS WITH WINGS

29

"A sower went out to sow his seed . . ."
(Luke 8:5)

As I was hiking with my two sons one Saturday morning, we noticed a number of large trees dispersing their seeds in a most fascinating way. The seeds were pea-sized with a single leaf-like extension about the size and shape of a large dragonfly wing. Under the weight of the seedpod, the single angled wing would cause the seed to fall with the perfect twirling, rotating motion of a helicopter. The effect was like the "paper helicopters" some of us used to make in elementary school. The seeds whirled around us, slowly descending from the tall trees, and often getting caught up in the breeze to be carried far from the parent tree. It was a delightful sight.

At one point, we climbed up a hill so that we could look out over the maples below. Amazingly, the wind was blowing some of the seeds upward from their trees of origin so that they would rise above the tallest branches, wafting on the wind for hundreds of yards until they landed on fields and pathways and rocks in the distance.

Jesus tells about a sower who goes out to sow, scattering seeds left and right, near and far. Some of the seeds fall on rocky paths, some are scooped up by hungry birds, and some are choked by weeds. But some find fertile soil, take root, and a harvest comes forth beyond what any of us can imagine. He tells the parable to remind us of the way our faithful efforts make a difference in the lives of others around us.

Watching the "seeds with wings," as my son called them, added a new dimension to Jesus' parable of the seeds and soils. So much of our impact, even when we live immensely fruitful lives, affects those closest to us. We are like trees whose seeds fall directly to the ground beneath their own branches and under their own shade. We naturally have the greatest impact upon those closest at hand, our families, spouses, children, and grandchildren. We bear much fruit this way, but in a narrow and limited field. The branches of trees that drop their seeds directly beneath them protect their seedlings, filter sunlight for their good, and provide fallen leaves to nurture them. Among the most important seeds we sow are the grace and love of God we offer within our own families and among our own kindred. This is our calling.

Each of us has another and larger calling as well, and that is to give our seeds wings so that the good we do and the difference we make extend beyond our sight and beyond our time.

Each of us has been formed by the influences of countless people—friends, coworkers, mentors, teachers, coaches, neighbors, pastors, youth sponsors, scout leaders, colleagues, confidants—who have contributed far beyond their own small circles. They have changed us, and changed the world, by intentionally providing a legacy that extends far and wide. I cannot begin to name all the hundreds of people who have significantly shaped who I am, how I think, what I believe, and how I live. These models and mentors and teachers have lived a faith that has transformed worlds, including my own.

I'm often amazed at the immeasurable difference people make with their lives far away from their homes and long after their deaths.

In Honduras, I'll see a clinic started by a Sunday school class from a church in Oklahoma many years ago. At a church camp, I'll notice the long list of donors whose combined efforts built a kitchen. At an inner city homeless shelter, I'll see a hand-carved cross and candlesticks given by a rural craftsman. In an African village, I'll see kids nestled under mosquito nets provided by youth from a church in Germany. In an American church, I see prayer cloths handmade by Christians in Korea. In nursing homes, I see birthday cards made by five-year-olds, and in church nurseries I find blankets knitted by the elderly homebound.

There is no end to what God can accomplish anywhere in the world when our "seeds have wings," when we are willing to let our prayers, intentions, plans, efforts, and work be lifted by the Spirit to places far away.

When we think about our own lives and the congregations of which we are part, consider where the seeds are falling. Just under our own feet, close to home? Or around the community, the country, the world?

I pray we bear much fruit, and that we scatter seeds not just in our own shadow but around the world. I pray for "seeds with wings."

Questions

- Think of two or three of the most influential people in forming your own soul and character other than your relatives. What made them effective? What can you learn from how they lived that will help you leave a legacy for others?
- Where in the world beyond your own church and home are there signs of your congregation's ministry? Of your own?

Prayer

Lift my eyes, dear God, and help me look beyond my own small world to a place far away where you call me to make a difference.

SOMEWHERE OUT THERE

30

"If you see some brother or sister in need and have the
means to do something about it but turn a cold shoulder
and do nothing, what happens to God's love? It disap-
pears. . . . My dear children, let's not just talk about love;
let's practice real love. This is the only way we'll know
we're living truly, living in God's reality."
(1 John 3:17-19, *THE MESSAGE*)

Somewhere out there is a five-year-old boy who doesn't know that right now plans are being made by a congregation he's never heard of to offer a neighborhood vacation Bible school that will change the direction of his life. The songs he will sing will stick in his mind, the stories of Jesus will enliven his imagination. The puppet show will make him laugh; the teacher will make him feel loved and welcomed; and the hospitality of those followers of Christ will so touch his mom and dad that they will take a small, unexpected step toward faith.

Somewhere out there is an elderly woman who feels like everyone has forgotten her. Her world has shrunk to her small apartment, the weekly trips to the grocery store, and the visits to the doctor's office. Her television has become her best friend. She doesn't know it, but right now a nearby congregation has awakened to the calling of God to invite people like her to a weekly lunch and to a chance to serve others. Soon she'll use her long-neglected skills to knit baby blankets that will wrap medical supplies bound for Central America, and this taste of community and purpose will save her life and give her a rebirth she never imagined possible.

Somewhere out there is a young couple stressed to the breaking point by personal debt. Fear squeezes the life out of them and fills their hearts with an unmitigated worry and an all-encompassing anxiety. The simple joy of shared companionship has given way to nonstop arguments about money. They don't know it, but one of their colleagues is praying for them, and asking God for the right words with which to invite them to come with her to a seminar at her church about managing money. The long path to new life and restored relationship will take them through the doors of a church they've never heard of and into a community that will shape them forever.

Somewhere out there is a teacher who thinks no one else cares about the children she has given her life to serving. Her schoolroom is rundown, and there's less money now than ever before to provide the resources she needs to do her job. She has no idea that a congregation is preparing themselves for a new ministry that will change her circumstances. Six months from now she will weep with joy as strangers repaint and refurbish her classroom. She cannot imagine that droves of people will step forward to volunteer to tutor, to read stories, and to coach basketball. She has no inkling of the effect this will have on her and on her students, and how this will open the door by which she rediscovers her own faith in Christ.

Somewhere out there is a young man whose inability to cope with the basic mechanisms of daily living has caused him to lose his job; to stop taking his meds; and to slip through the cracks of every social, community, and family network. He kept falling and falling until now he sleeps on the streets, carries cardboard for bedding, and digs through trash for dinner. He has no idea that a congregation is gearing up to offer a soup kitchen, and that this ministry will change his life. He cannot imagine that as he is served a meal, someone will engage him in conversation, treat him as human, listen to his story, learn his name, and reconnect him to his family and to the social networks that will allow him to live again a basic life with dignity. He has no idea that God, working through people desiring to follow Christ, will restore him to a life he barely remembers.

Somewhere out there in an African village a young girl and her little sister read stories together in bed, both of them safely protected by a mosquito net bought by the youth of a rural church in the Midwest. No one can see it now, but she will grow up to become a doctor, relieving the suffering of thousands. She will live a full life that never would have been possible without a simple net and many generous young hearts across the globe.

People ask me what I hope happens when a congregation focuses on the Five Practices. When I picture success, I don't see smiling pastors with good preaching material or church committees with well-developed strategic plans—as important as these are.

I imagine that somewhere out there, somewhere in Texas or California or Virginia or Michigan or Mozambique, somewhere in a town like yours or a neighborhood near you is a person who has no idea of the change that is coming his way or the grace that will transform her. I picture the person unknowingly prepared by the Spirit of God to receive the embrace of Christ that people will offer when they come alive with purpose and fulfill the mission of Christ.

Somewhere out there is a person God plans to use you to reach. Somewhere out there is a person God will use to change your life as you reach them. Somewhere out there is a person for whom Christ died, and for whom your church was built, and for whom God has uniquely prepared you to reach.

PREACHING OUT

Questions

- Who are some of the "somewhere out there" people you and your congregation are reaching?
- Who are you uniquely qualified and perfectly situated to touch with the grace and ministry of Christ whom no one else can possibly reach?

Prayer

Lord, may I not miss the person you have prepared me to reach on your behalf, and not fail the calling you have given me in Christ.